D0990852

THE U.S. CONSTITUTION AND CONSTITUTIONAL LAW

GOVERNANCE: POWER, POLITICS, AND PARTICIPATION

THE U.S. CONSTITUTION AND CONSTITUTIONAL LAW

EDITED BY BRIAN DUIGNAN, SENIOR EDITOR, RELIGION AND PHILOSOPHY

Published in 2013 by Britannica Educational Publishing
(a trademark of Encyclopædia Britannica, Inc.)
in association with Rosen Educational Services, LLC
29 East 21st Street, New York, NY 10010.

Distributed exclusively by Rosen Educational Services.
For a listing of additional Britannica Educational Publishing titles, call toll free (800) 237-9932.

First Edition

Library of Congress Cataloging-in-Publication Data

The U.S. Constitution and constitutional law/edited by Brian Duignan.
p. cm.—(Governance: Power, Politics, and Participation)
"In association with Britannica Publishing, Rosen Educational Services."
Includes bibliographical references and index.
ISBN 978-1-61530-688-6 (library binding)
1. Constitutional amendments—United States. 2. Constitutional law—United States. 3. Constituent power—United States. 4. Federal government—United States. 5. Civil rights—United States. I. Duignan, Brian. II. Title: United States Constitution and constitutional law.
KF4557.D85 2013
342.7302—dc23

2011046550

Manufactured in the United States of America

On the cover, pp. i, iii (top) The U.S. Constitution, which took effect in 1789, is now the oldest written constitution in the world. © *www.istockphoto.com/Alan Crosthwaite*

On the cover (centre), pp. i (centre), iii (centre), 1, 13, 52, 109, 143, 145, 175, 179, 181 Columns that make up the portico of the United States Supreme Court. © *www.istockphoto.com/Jeremy Edwards*

On the cover, pp. i, iii (bottom) Occupy Wall Street demonstrators, exercising their right to engage in civil disobedience, display signs in New York City's Zuccotti Park, Oct. 7, 2011. A privately-owned public space which became the main staging ground for OWS, the park was cleared of protestors by the New York Police Department Nov. 17, 2011. *Hope Lourie Killcoyne*

CONTENTS

14

21

23

59
68
THE FIFTEENTH AMENDMENT
80

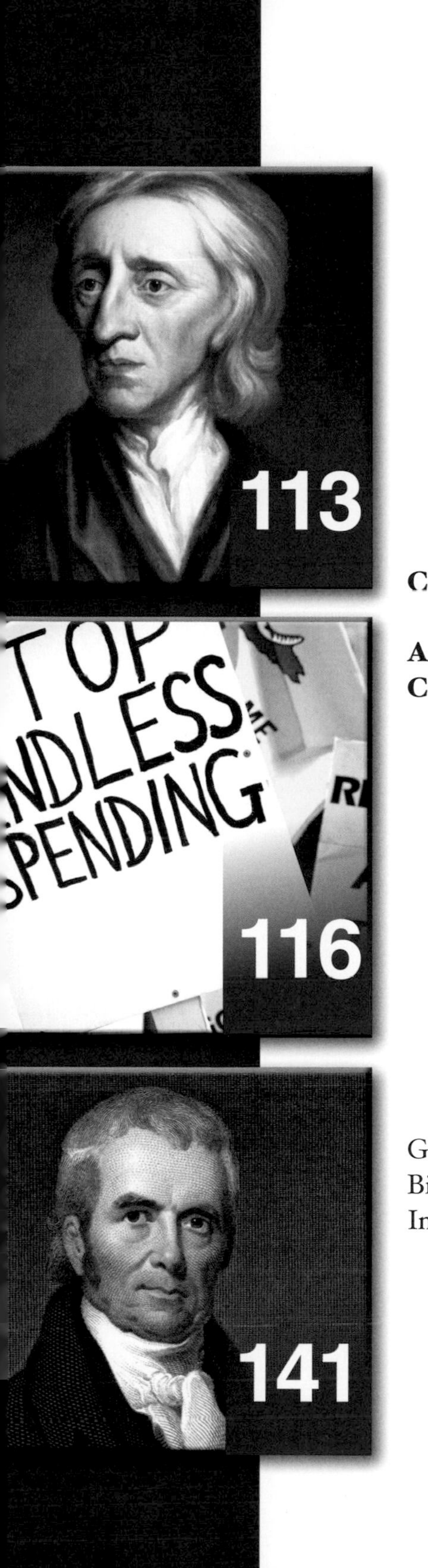
113
116
141

INTRODUCTION

The United States Constitution, ratified in 1787, is the oldest written constitution still in use and is a landmark document of the Western world. For more than two centuries, democratic movements around the world have looked to the principles enshrined in it as they've struggled for freedom. At less than 5,000 words for its seven articles and 27 amendments, it is also among the shortest of the written constitutions used in the world; by comparison, India's constitution runs well over 100,000 words for its more than 400 articles and nearly 100 amendments. This brevity has its virtues, as the Constitution can adapt to changing historical circumstances, but, even for

Two protestors from the Occupy Wall Street movement use signs to exercise their constitutionally protected right to express their opinions regarding the banking industry, New York, N.Y., Oct. 17, 2011. The movement, which first established itself in New York City's Zuccotti Park in the Wall Street financial district Sept. 17, 2011, sparked a host of like-minded demonstrations nationwide. Hope Lourie Killcoyne

constitutional scholars, the vagueness of many of the articles also means that it is not always clear what it actually means.

Article VI stipulates clearly, "This Constitution…shall be the supreme Law of the Land; and the Judges in every State shall be bound thereby." This "supremacy clause" sounds quite simple and straightforward, but in practice historically it has been anything but.

The First Amendment, for example, states, in part, that "Congress shall make no law…abridging the freedom of speech, or of the press." But a mere 11 years after the Constitution was ratified, the U.S. Congress passed a series of laws that severely restricted the freedom of the press. One such law, the Sedition Act, passed in July 1798, made it illegal to publish false or malicious writings against the government or to incite any opposition to the president or to laws passed by Congress. To 21st century sensibilities, particularly in the context of the Tea Party movement that flourished beginning in 2009 and the Occupy Wall Street movement that sprang up in 2011, this seems quite at odds with the constitutional liberties we take for granted.

Likewise, the Constitution gives the federal government power over interstate commerce. Found in Article I, Section 8, the commerce clause is the legal foundation of much of the federal government's regulatory authority and has traditionally allowed the federal government broad latitude in enacting new regulations. That said, does the clause give the federal government the power to mandate that an individual purchase health care insurance, as required in the sweeping health care reform bill, the Affordable Care Act, passed into law in 2010? Some constitutional experts say yes, basing their opinion in part on the commerce clause, but also on the broad "necessary and proper clause" found in the very same Article I, Section 8, which gives Congress the power "To make all Laws which shall be necessary and proper for carrying into Execution the foregoing Powers, and all other Powers vested by this Constitution in the Government of the United States." But, these constitutional scholars also point to the Preamble to the Constitution, which asserts the "general welfare" of the citizens of the United States as a founding responsibility of the federal government, suggesting that the Affordable Care Act was a permissible exertion of constitutional authority by Congress. Meanwhile, other constitutional experts assert that Congress may only regulate economic activity—rather than inactivity—and thus they view requiring individuals to purchase health care as going well beyond those powers vested in Congress. And further, that even if Congress might believe that the requirement is "necessary", it may not be a "proper" exercise of legislative authority.

The preceding argument highlights just two specific controversies in the recent and distant past, but it crystallizes the essence of constitutional debate in the United States. Constitutional experts disagree over the meaning of the Constitution, and even the interpretation of what the individual clauses mean in the Constitution changes over time, depending on not only the political complexion of the justices on the Supreme Court but also any general consensus that might exist in society.

The U.S. Constitution was drawn up at a Constitutional Convention in Philadelphia beginning on May 25, 1787. The convention was precipitated by Shays's Rebellion (August 1786–February 1787), which highlighted both the weaknesses of the central government under the Articles of Confederation (the country's first Constitution) as well as the severe economic troubles of the day. Once gathered in Philadelphia, the delegates to the convention, ostensibly there to amend the Articles of Confederation, instead almost immediately set about the task of writing a new constitution.

After several months of intense negotiations and disagreements during a long hot summer in Philadelphia, the final document was signed on Sept. 17 by 39 of the 55 delegates who participated in the proceedings. Although sometimes we attribute an almost divine hand in the crafting of the Constitution, the document itself was a product of compromise and, as the signature tally implies, was not universally accepted by all of the Founding Fathers. Indeed, at Virginia's ratifying convention in 1788, the statesman Patrick Henry announced his opposition, objecting even to the first three words of the Constitution's Preamble: "We the People." For Henry and other critics, the Constitution was an affront to states' rights, and the principles enshrined in it were "extremely pernicious, impolitic, and dangerous."

Among the most important compromises made at Philadelphia was over the balance of power between the states and the federal government. A group of small states introduced a plan that would provide equal representation, while the large states called for representation based on population. In the end, in what has been termed the "Great Compromise", the legislative branch of the United States was split into two equally powerful chambers: one, the House of Representatives, would be based on population, while the other, the Senate, would provide equal representation to each state.

But who counted as a person for representation? While some delegates wanted to abolish slavery entirely, doing so was impossible if a union was to be formed. Southern delegates wanted slaves counted for representation purposes, while Northern delegates wanted only the free population enumerated. In the end, a three-fifths compromise was struck, a bit of bizarre calculus in which slaves were counted as three-fifths of a person, thus boosting in the House of Representatives the influence of the Southern states. To forestall a further breakdown of the Constitutional Convention, the final document also forbade Congress from regulating the slave trade for 20 years, thus pushing off conflict over slavery for another set of leaders.

The ratification of the Constitution was not a foregone conclusion. Passage in New York seemed especially critical, and three supporters of the Constitution—Alexander Hamilton (who would become the first secretary of the Treasury), John Jay (who would become the first chief justice of the United States), and James Madison (the chief architect of the Constitution and the country's fourth president)—published, under the pseudonym "Publius," a series of essays known as the Federalist Papers that was a masterful defense of the new Constitution and helped secure New York's ratification. By June 1788 the new Constitution had been ratified by the requisite nine states, but in many states, passage was predicated on an enactment of a Bill of Rights—what would become the first 10 amendments to the Constitution—and those were certified on Dec. 15, 1791.

The Bill of Rights provides limits on federal authority and

protects the rights of individuals and the states, some which are particularly relevant today. They include freedom of religion, the press, speech, and assembly (First Amendment); the right to keep and bear arms (Second); freedom from unreasonable search and seizure (Fourth); protections against double jeopardy and being forced to testify against oneself and prohibitions of the taking of life, liberty, or property without due process of law (Fifth); a right to a speedy public trial by jury (Sixth); and prohibitions on excessive bail and cruel and unusual punishments (Eighth). The Tenth Amendment enshrines states' rights into the Constitution, stipulating that "powers not delegated to the United States by the Constitution, nor prohibited by it to the States, are reserved to the States respectively, or to the people." But what exactly is a power reserved to the states, and how does that mesh with the necessary and proper clause that provides broad authority to the federal government? And who decides that question? The answer lies in the principles underlying the Constitution.

The Constitution established a republican form of government and was based on the principles of checks and balances and separation of powers. That is, the three branches of government—executive, legislative, and judicial—had certain responsibilities delegated to them, but to ensure that no branch of government would become all powerful, the Constitution embedded ways in which each branch could oversee the other. For example, while lawmaking authority is concentrated in the legislative branch, the president can veto, or reject, a bill, but if there is overwhelming support for legislation, Congress may override this veto by the president by a two-thirds vote. Likewise, while the president is commander-in-chief of the armed forces, the power to declare war is vested in Congress (though how much military activity the president can pursue short of a formal declaration of war has been a point of controversy, particularly since the era of the Vietnam War).

The Supreme Court can check the powers of the legislative

and executive branches by invalidating laws or declaring actions by the executive branch unconstitutional through what is called judicial review. But where exactly is this power found in the Constitution? Surprisingly, though it is implied, judicial review is never explicitly granted to the Supreme Court. Rather, it was established through a case brought before the Supreme Court in 1803, *Marbury* v. *Madison*, in which the Supreme Court invalidated a section of the Federal Judiciary Act of 1789. The exercise of this power was not without controversy, though there was little effective political challenge to it, and over time the history of constitutional law in the United States largely became a history of Supreme Court decisions.

Since the Supreme Court is the ultimate arbiter of what is valid under the Constitution, it would seem that it is perhaps the most powerful branch of government. Still, the Supreme Court's power is also subject to checks and balances. Most important, of course, the president appoints judges to vacant seats on the Supreme Court and other federal courts, and those appointments must be approved by a majority of the Senate. The ultimate check on the Supreme Court, however, is a constitutional amendment that would effectively override a Supreme Court decision. Because it generally takes a two-thirds vote in each house of Congress, plus the support of three-fourths of state legislatures, it is not simple to pass a constitutional amendment—there have only been 17 amendments since the Bill of Rights was enacted.

As the examples of freedom of the press and speech and health care noted earlier suggest, what the Constitution means is not cut-and-dry, and constitutional experts often disagree over the precise meaning of clauses and amendments. Those disputes often have been resolved by the U.S. Supreme Court—but even the Supreme Court has reversed previous decisions. For example, in 1896 in *Plessy* v. *Ferguson*, the Supreme Court established the "separate but equal" doctrine, whereby racial segregation was deemed permissible. Fifty-eight years later, the Supreme Court reversed this ruling in *Brown* v. *Board of Education*, declaring racial segregation unconstitutional.

On controversial and often emotional issues, the Supreme Court has played a vital role. Its 1857 *Dred Scott* decision, in which the Court ruled in effect that slavery was legal in all U.S. territories, helped propel the United States into civil war just four years later. In 1895 the Court held that a federal income tax was unconstitutional—a ruling later invalidated by the adoption of the Sixteenth Amendment. In 1944, during World War II, the Court held in *Korematsu* v. *United States* that the internment of U.S. citizens of Japanese descent was permissible. In 1966 in *Miranda* v. *Arizona*, the Court required that the police inform arrested persons of their rights, including the right to remain silent. In 1973 the Court ruled that states could not unduly restrict abortion rights in *Roe* v. *Wade*. In 1989, in *Texas* v. *Johnson*, the Court held that burning the U.S. flag was constitutionally protected free speech. In 2000, in *Bush* v. *Gore*, the Supreme Court's ruling that halted a manual recount of ballots in Florida effectively awarded the presidency to George W. Bush. In 2008, in *District of Columbia* v. *Heller*, the Court ruled that the Second Amendment guaranteed individuals the right to possess firearms independent of service in a state militia and to use firearms for traditionally lawful purposes, including self-defense within the home. And in 2010, in *Citizens United* v. *Federal Election Commission*, the Supreme Court declared that laws preventing corporations and unions from using general treasury funds for independent electioneering communications were an undue violation of free speech.

Nearly infinite other judicial decisions could be cited—ranging from capital punishment to property rights; these examples are used to underscore the breadth covered under the rubric of constitutional law and the real-world importance of the workings of the Supreme Court and the federal court system that you will encounter in this volume.

CHAPTER 1

The Constitution of the United States

The Constitution of the United States is the fundamental law of the U.S. federal system of government and a landmark document of the Western world. The oldest written national constitution in use, the Constitution defines the principal organs of government and their jurisdictions and the basic rights of citizens.

THE CONSTITUTIONAL CONVENTION

The Constitution was written during the summer of 1787 in Philadelphia by 55 delegates to a Constitutional Convention that was called ostensibly to amend the Articles of Confederation (1781–89), the country's first written constitution. The Constitution was the product of political compromise after long and often rancorous debates over issues such as states' rights, representation, and slavery. Delegates from small and large states disagreed over whether the number of representatives in the new federal legislature should be the same for each state—as was the case under the Articles of Confederation—or different depending on a state's population. In addition, some delegates from Northern states sought to abolish slavery or, failing that, to make representation dependent on the size of a state's free population. At the same time, some Southern delegates threatened to abandon the convention if their demands to keep slavery and the slave trade legal and to count slaves for representation purposes were not met. Eventually the framers resolved their disputes by adopting a proposal put forward by the Connecticut delegation. The Great Compromise, as it came to be known, created a bicameral legislature with a Senate, in which all states would be equally represented, and a House of Representatives, in which representation would be apportioned on the basis of a state's free population plus three-fifths of its slave population. (The inclusion of the slave population was known separately as the three-fifths compromise.) A further compromise on slavery prohibited Congress from banning the importation of slaves until 1808 (Article I, Section 9). After all the disagreements were bridged, the new Constitution was submitted for ratification to the 13 states on Sept. 28, 1787. In 1787–88, in an effort to persuade New York to ratify the Constitution, Alexander Hamilton, John Jay, and James Madison published a series of essays on the Constitution and republican government in New York newspapers. Their work, written under the pseudonym "Publius" and collected and published in book form as *The Federalist* (1788), became a classic exposition and defense of the Constitution. In June 1788, after the Constitution had been ratified by nine states (as required by Article VII), Congress set March 4, 1789, as the date for the new government to commence proceedings (the first elections under the Constitution were held late in 1788). Because ratification in many states was contingent on the promised addition of a Bill of Rights, Congress proposed 12 amendments in September 1789; 10 were ratified by the states, and their adoption was certified on Dec. 15, 1791. (One of the original 12 proposed amendments, which prohibited midterm changes in compensation for members of Congress, was ratified in 1992 as the Twenty-seventh Amendment. The last one, concerning the ratio of citizens per member of the House of Representatives, has never been adopted.)

The authors of the Constitution were heavily influenced by the country's experience under the Articles of Confederation, which had attempted to retain as much independence and sovereignty for the states as possible and to assign to the central government only those nationally important functions that the states could not handle individually. But the events of the years 1781 to 1787, including the national government's inability to act during Shays's Rebellion, an armed revolt of debtors in Massachusetts (1786–87), showed that the Articles were unworkable because they deprived the national government of many essential powers, including direct taxation and the ability to regulate interstate commerce. It was hoped that the new Constitution would remedy this problem.

The framers of the Constitution were especially concerned with limiting the power of government and securing the liberty of citizens. The doctrine of legislative, executive, and judicial separation of powers, the checks and balances of each branch against the others, and the explicit guarantees of individual liberty were all designed to strike a balance between authority and liberty—the central purpose of American constitutional law.

PROVISIONS OF THE CONSTITUTION

The Constitution concisely organizes the country's basic political institutions. The main text comprises seven articles. Article I vests all legislative powers in the Congress—the House of Representatives and the Senate. The Great Compromise stipulated that representation in the House would be based on population, and each state is entitled to two senators. Members of the House serve terms of two years, senators terms of six. Among the powers delegated to Congress are the right to levy taxes, borrow money, regulate interstate commerce, provide for military

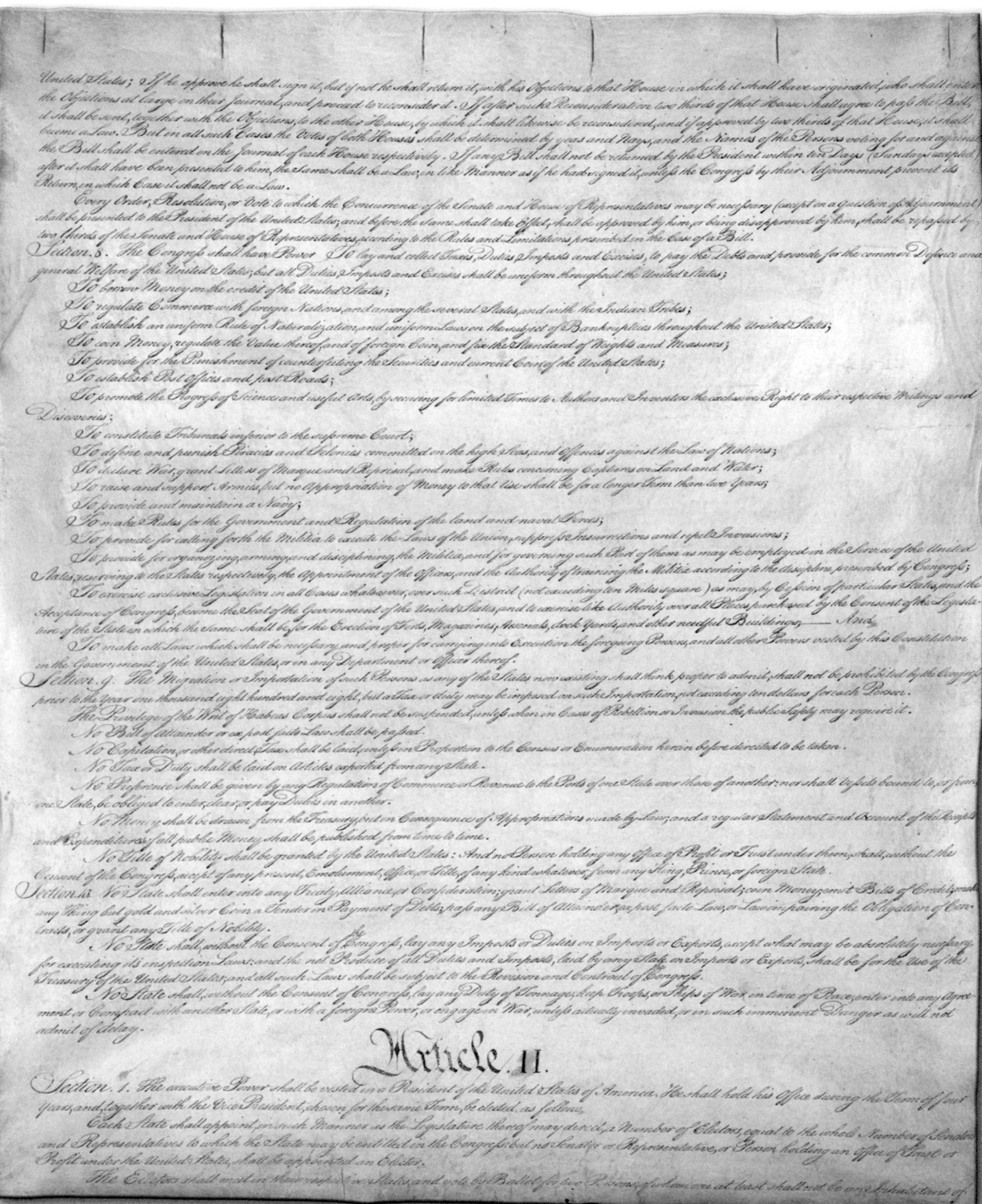

United States; If he approve he shall sign it, but if not he shall return it, with his Objections to that House in which it shall have originated, who shall enter the Objections at large on their Journal, and proceed to reconsider it. If after such Reconsideration two thirds of that House shall agree to pass the Bill, it shall be sent, together with the Objections, to the other House, by which it shall likewise be reconsidered, and if approved by two thirds of that House, it shall become a Law. But in all such Cases the Votes of both Houses shall be determined by yeas and Nays, and the Names of the Persons voting for and against the Bill shall be entered on the Journal of each House respectively. If any Bill shall not be returned by the President within ten Days (Sundays excepted) after it shall have been presented to him, the Same shall be a Law, in like Manner as if he had signed it, unless the Congress by their Adjournment prevent its Return, in which Case it shall not be a Law.

Every Order, Resolution, or Vote to which the Concurrence of the Senate and House of Representatives may be necessary (except on a question of Adjournment) shall be presented to the President of the United States; and before the Same shall take Effect, shall be approved by him, or being disapproved by him, shall be repassed by two thirds of the Senate and House of Representatives, according to the Rules and Limitations prescribed in the Case of a Bill.

Section. 8. The Congress shall have Power To lay and collect Taxes, Duties, Imposts and Excises, to pay the Debts and provide for the common Defence and general Welfare of the United States; but all Duties, Imposts and Excises shall be uniform throughout the United States;

To borrow Money on the credit of the United States;

To regulate Commerce with foreign Nations, and among the several States, and with the Indian Tribes;

To establish an uniform Rule of Naturalization, and uniform Laws on the subject of Bankruptcies throughout the United States;

To coin Money, regulate the Value thereof, and of foreign Coin, and fix the Standard of Weights and Measures;

To provide for the Punishment of counterfeiting the Securities and current Coin of the United States;

To establish Post Offices and post Roads;

To promote the Progress of Science and useful Arts, by securing for limited Times to Authors and Inventors the exclusive Right to their respective Writings and Discoveries;

To constitute Tribunals inferior to the supreme Court;

To define and punish Piracies and Felonies committed on the high Seas, and Offences against the Law of Nations;

To declare War, grant Letters of Marque and Reprisal, and make Rules concerning Captures on Land and Water;

To raise and support Armies, but no Appropriation of Money to that Use shall be for a longer Term than two Years;

To provide and maintain a Navy;

To make Rules for the Government and Regulation of the land and naval Forces;

To provide for calling forth the Militia to execute the Laws of the Union, suppress Insurrections and repel Invasions;

To provide for organizing, arming, and disciplining, the Militia, and for governing such Part of them as may be employed in the Service of the United States, reserving to the States respectively, the Appointment of the Officers, and the Authority of training the Militia according to the discipline prescribed by Congress;

To exercise exclusive Legislation in all Cases whatsoever, over such District (not exceeding ten Miles square) as may, by Cession of particular States, and the Acceptance of Congress, become the Seat of the Government of the United States, and to exercise like Authority over all Places purchased by the Consent of the Legislature of the State in which the Same shall be, for the Erection of Forts, Magazines, Arsenals, dock-Yards, and other needful Buildings;—And

To make all Laws which shall be necessary and proper for carrying into Execution the foregoing Powers, and all other Powers vested by this Constitution in the Government of the United States, or in any Department or Officer thereof.

Section. 9. The Migration or Importation of such Persons as any of the States now existing shall think proper to admit, shall not be prohibited by the Congress prior to the Year one thousand eight hundred and eight, but a Tax or duty may be imposed on such Importation, not exceeding ten dollars for each Person.

The Privilege of the Writ of Habeas Corpus shall not be suspended, unless when in Cases of Rebellion or Invasion the public Safety may require it.

No Bill of Attainder or ex post facto Law shall be passed.

No Capitation, or other direct, Tax shall be laid, unless in Proportion to the Census or Enumeration herein before directed to be taken.

No Tax or Duty shall be laid on Articles exported from any State.

No Preference shall be given by any Regulation of Commerce or Revenue to the Ports of one State over those of another: nor shall Vessels bound to, or from, one State, be obliged to enter, clear, or pay Duties in another.

No Money shall be drawn from the Treasury, but in Consequence of Appropriations made by Law; and a regular Statement and Account of the Receipts and Expenditures of all public Money shall be published from time to time.

No Title of Nobility shall be granted by the United States: And no Person holding any Office of Profit or Trust under them, shall, without the Consent of the Congress, accept of any present, Emolument, Office, or Title, of any kind whatever, from any King, Prince, or foreign State.

Section. 10. No State shall enter into any Treaty, Alliance, or Confederation; grant Letters of Marque and Reprisal; coin Money; emit Bills of Credit; make any Thing but gold and silver Coin a Tender in Payment of Debts; pass any Bill of Attainder, ex post facto Law, or Law impairing the Obligation of Contracts, or grant any Title of Nobility.

No State shall, without the Consent of the Congress, lay any Imposts or Duties on Imports or Exports, except what may be absolutely necessary for executing its inspection Laws: and the net Produce of all Duties and Imposts, laid by any State on Imports or Exports, shall be for the Use of the Treasury of the United States; and all such Laws shall be subject to the Revision and Controul of the Congress.

No State shall, without the Consent of Congress, lay any Duty of Tonnage, keep Troops, or Ships of War in time of Peace, enter into any Agreement or Compact with another State, or with a foreign Power, or engage in War, unless actually invaded, or in such imminent Danger as will not admit of delay.

Article. II.

Section. 1. The executive Power shall be vested in a President of the United States of America. He shall hold his Office during the Term of four Years, and, together with the Vice President, chosen for the same Term, be elected, as follows

Each State shall appoint, in such Manner as the Legislature thereof may direct, a Number of Electors, equal to the whole Number of Senators and Representatives to which the State may be entitled in the Congress: but no Senator or Representative, or Person holding an Office of Trust or Profit under the United States, shall be appointed an Elector.

The Electors shall meet in their respective States, and vote by Ballot for two Persons, of whom one at least shall not be an Inhabitant of

The opening lines of Article II on the second page of the Constitution of the United States of America. NARA

forces, declare war, and determine member seating and rules of procedure. The House initiates impeachment proceedings, and the Senate adjudicates them.

Article II vests executive power in the office of the presidency of the United States. The president, selected by an electoral college to serve a four-year term, is given responsibilities common to chief executives, including serving as commander-in-chief of the armed forces, negotiating treaties (two-thirds of the Senate must concur), and granting pardons. The president's vast appointment powers, which include members of the federal judiciary and the cabinet, are subject to the "advice and consent" (majority approval) of the Senate (Article II, Section 2). Originally presidents were eligible for continual reelection, but the Twenty-second Amendment (1951) later prohibited any person from being elected president more than twice. Although the formal powers of the president are constitutionally quite limited and vague in comparison with those of Congress, a variety of historical and technological factors—such as the centralization of power in the executive branch during war and the advent of television—have increased the informal responsibilities of the office extensively to embrace other aspects of political leadership, including proposing legislation to Congress.

Article III places judicial power in the hands of the courts. The Constitution is interpreted by the courts, and the Supreme Court of the United States is the final court of appeal from the state and lower federal courts. The power of American courts to rule on the constitutionality of laws, known as judicial review, is held by few other courts in the world and is not explicitly granted in the Constitution. The principle of judicial review was first asserted by Supreme Court Chief Justice John Marshall in *Marbury* v. *Madison* (1803), when the court ruled that it had the authority to void national or state laws.

Article III and the opening line of Article IV on the third page of the Constitution of the United States of America. NARA

Beyond the body of judicial rulings interpreting it, the Constitution acquires meaning in a broader sense at the hands of all who use it. Congress on innumerable occasions has given new scope to the document through statutes, such as those creating executive departments, the federal courts, territories, and states; controlling succession to the presidency; and setting up the executive budget system. The chief executive also has contributed to constitutional interpretation, as in the development of the executive agreement as an instrument of foreign policy. Practices outside the letter of the Constitution based on custom and usage are often recognized as constitutional elements; they include the system of political parties, presidential nomination procedures, and the conduct of election campaigns. The presidential cabinet is largely a constitutional "convention" based on custom, and the actual operation of the electoral college system is also a convention.

Article IV deals, in part, with relations between the states and privileges of the citizens of the states. These provisions include the full faith and credit clause, which requires states to recognize the official acts and judicial proceedings of other states; the requirement that each state provide citizens from other states with all the privileges and immunities afforded the citizens of that state; and the guarantee of a republican form of government for each state. Article V stipulates the procedures for amending the Constitution. Amendments may be proposed by a two-thirds vote of both houses of Congress or by a convention called by Congress on the application of the legislatures of two-thirds of the states. Proposed amendments must be ratified by three-fourths of the state legislatures or by conventions in as many states, depending on the decision of Congress. All subsequent amendments have been proposed by Congress, and all but one—the

Congress may by general Laws prescribe the Manner in which such Acts, Records and Proceedings shall be proved, and the Effect thereof.

Section. 2. The Citizens of each State shall be entitled to all Privileges and Immunities of Citizens in the several States.

A Person charged in any State with Treason, Felony, or other Crime, who shall flee from Justice, and be found in another State, shall on Demand of the executive Authority of the State from which he fled, be delivered up, to be removed to the State having Jurisdiction of the Crime.

No Person held to Service or Labour in one State, under the Laws thereof, escaping into another, shall, in Consequence of any Law or Regulation therein, be discharged from such Service or Labour, but shall be delivered up on Claim of the Party to whom such Service or Labour may be due.

Section. 3. New States may be admitted by the Congress into this Union; but no new State shall be formed or erected within the Jurisdiction of any other State; nor any State be formed by the Junction of two or more States, or Parts of States, without the Consent of the Legislatures of the States concerned as well as of the Congress.

The Congress shall have Power to dispose of and make all needful Rules and Regulations respecting the Territory or other Property belonging to the United States; and nothing in this Constitution shall be so construed as to Prejudice any Claims of the United States, or of any particular State.

Section. 4. The United States shall guarantee to every State in this Union a Republican Form of Government, and shall protect each of them against Invasion; and on Application of the Legislature, or of the Executive (when the Legislature cannot be convened) against domestic Violence.

Article. V.

The Congress, whenever two thirds of both Houses shall deem it necessary, shall propose Amendments to this Constitution, or, on the Application of the Legislatures of two thirds of the several States, shall call a Convention for proposing Amendments, which, in either Case, shall be valid to all Intents and Purposes, as Part of this Constitution, when ratified by the Legislatures of three fourths of the several States, or by Conventions in three fourths thereof, as the one or the other Mode of Ratification may be proposed by the Congress; Provided that no Amendment which may be made prior to the Year One thousand eight hundred and eight shall in any Manner affect the first and fourth Clauses in the Ninth Section of the first Article; and that no State, without its Consent, shall be deprived of its equal Suffrage in the Senate.

Article. VI.

All Debts contracted and Engagements entered into, before the Adoption of this Constitution, shall be as valid against the United States under this Constitution, as under the Confederation.

This Constitution, and the Laws of the United States which shall be made in Pursuance thereof; and all Treaties made, or which shall be made, under the Authority of the United States, shall be the supreme Law of the Land; and the Judges in every State shall be bound thereby, any Thing in the Constitution or Laws of any State to the Contrary notwithstanding.

The Senators and Representatives before mentioned, and the Members of the several State Legislatures, and all executive and judicial Officers, both of the United States and of the several States, shall be bound by Oath or Affirmation, to support this Constitution; but no religious Test shall ever be required as a Qualification to any Office or public Trust under the United States.

Article. VII.

The Ratification of the Conventions of nine States, shall be sufficient for the Establishment of this Constitution between the States so ratifying the Same.

The Word, "the," being interlined between the seventh and eighth Lines of the first Page, The Word "Thirty" being partly written on an Erazure in the fifteenth Line of the first Page, The Words "is tried" being interlined between the thirty second and thirty third Lines of the first Page and the Word "the" being interlined between the forty third and forty fourth Lines of the second Page.

Attest William Jackson Secretary

done in Convention by the Unanimous Consent of the States present the Seventeenth Day of September in the Year of our Lord one thousand seven hundred and Eighty seven and of the Independance of the United States of America the Twelfth In witness whereof We have hereunto subscribed our Names,

G° Washington—Presid^t and deputy from Virginia

Delaware: Geo: Read, Gunning Bedford jun, John Dickinson, Richard Bassett, Jaco: Broom

Maryland: James McHenry, Dan of St Thos Jenifer, Danl Carroll

Virginia: John Blair—, James Madison Jr.

North Carolina: Wm Blount, Richd Dobbs Spaight, Hu Williamson

South Carolina: J. Rutledge, Charles Cotesworth Pinckney, Charles Pinckney, Pierce Butler

Georgia: William Few, Abr Baldwin

New Hampshire: John Langdon, Nicholas Gilman

Massachusetts: Nathaniel Gorham, Rufus King

Connecticut: Wm Saml Johnson, Roger Sherman

New York: Alexander Hamilton

New Jersey: Wil: Livingston, David Brearley, Wm Paterson, Jona: Dayton

Pensylvania: B Franklin, Thomas Mifflin, Robt Morris, Geo. Clymer, Thos FitzSimons, Jared Ingersoll, James Wilson, Gouv Morris

Articles V, VI, and VII on the last page of the Constitution of the United States of America. NARA

Twenty-first Amendment, which repealed Prohibition (the Eighteenth Amendment)—have been ratified by state legislatures.

Article VI, which prohibits religious tests for officeholders, also deals with public debts and the supremacy of the Constitution, citing the document as "the supreme Law of the Land;...any Thing in the Constitution or Laws of any State to the Contrary notwithstanding." Article VII stipulated that the Constitution would become operational after being ratified by nine states.

The national government has only those constitutional powers that are delegated to it either expressly or by implication; the states, unless otherwise restricted, possess all the remaining powers (Tenth Amendment). Thus, national powers are enumerated (Article I, Section 8, paragraphs 1–17), and state powers are not. The state powers are often called residual, or reserved, powers. The elastic, or necessary and proper, clause (Article I, Section 8, paragraph 18) states that Congress shall have the authority "To make all Laws which shall be necessary and proper for carrying into Execution" the various powers vested in the national government. Thus, it follows that, in addition to the delegated powers, Congress possesses implied powers, a proposition established by Chief Justice Marshall in *McCulloch* v. *Maryland* (1819). The issue of national versus state power was not fully resolved by this decision, however, and many political battles in American history—including debates on nullification, slavery, racial segregation, and abortion—often have been disputes over constitutional interpretations of implied and residual powers.

Competing concepts of federal supremacy and states' rights were brought into sharp relief in questions about commercial regulation. The commerce clause simply authorized Congress "To regulate Commerce with foreign Nations, and among the several States, and with the Indian Tribes." Particularly since a series of decisions in 1937, the Court has interpreted Congress's regulatory power broadly under the commerce clause as new methods of interstate transportation and communication have come into use. States may not regulate any aspect of interstate commerce that Congress has preempted.

ELECTORAL COLLEGE

The electoral college is a constitutionally mandated process for electing the U.S. president and vice president. Each state appoints as many electors as it has senators and representatives in Congress (U.S. senators, representatives, and government officers are ineligible); the District of Columbia has three votes. A winner-takes-all rule operates in every state except Maine and Nebraska. Three presidents have been elected by means of an electoral college victory while losing the national popular vote (Rutherford B. Hayes in 1877, Benjamin Harrison in 1888, and George W. Bush in 2000). Although pledged to vote for their state's winners, electors are not constitutionally obliged to do so. A candidate must win 270 of the 538 votes to win the election.

CIVIL LIBERTIES AND THE BILL OF RIGHTS

The federal government is obliged by many constitutional provisions to respect the individual citizen's basic rights. Some civil liberties were specified in the original document, notably in the provisions guaranteeing the writ of habeas corpus and trial by jury in criminal cases (Article III, Section 2) and forbidding bills of attainder and ex post facto laws (Article I, Section 9). But the most significant limitations to government's power over the individual were added in 1791 in the Bill of Rights. The Constitution's First Amendment guarantees the rights of conscience—such as freedom of religion, speech, and the press—and the right of peaceful assembly and petition. Other guarantees in the Bill of Rights require fair procedures for persons accused of a crime—such as protection against unreasonable search and seizure, compulsory self-incrimination, double jeopardy, and excessive bail—and guarantees of a speedy and public trial by a local, impartial jury before an impartial judge and representation by counsel. Rights of private property are also guaranteed. Although the Bill of Rights is a broad expression of individual civil liberties, the ambiguous wording of many of its provisions—such as the Second Amendment's right "to keep and bear Arms" and the Eighth Amendment's prohibition of "cruel and unusual punishments"—has been a source of constitutional controversy and intense political debate. Further, the rights guaranteed are not absolute, and there has been considerable disagreement about the extent to which they limit governmental authority. The Bill of Rights originally protected citizens only from the national government. For example, although the Constitution prohibited the establishment of an official religion at the national level, the official state-supported religion of Massachusetts was Congregationalism until 1833. Thus, individual citizens had to look to state constitutions for protection of their rights against state governments, a less than ideal situation.

THE FOURTEENTH AMENDMENT: DUE PROCESS AND EQUAL PROTECTION CLAUSES

After the American Civil War, three new constitutional amendments were adopted: the Thirteenth, which abolished slavery; the Fourteenth, which granted citizenship to former slaves; and the Fifteenth, which guaranteed former male slaves the right to vote. The Fourteenth Amendment placed an important federal limitation on the states by forbidding them to deny to any person "life, liberty, or property, without due process of law" and guaranteeing every person within a state's jurisdiction "the equal protection of its laws." Later interpretations by the Supreme Court in the 20th century gave these two clauses added significance. In *Gitlow* v. *New York* (1925), the due process clause was interpreted by the Supreme Court to broaden the applicability of the Bill of Rights' protection of speech to the states, holding both levels of government to the same constitutional standard. During subsequent decades, the Supreme Court selectively applied the due process clause to protect other liberties guaranteed in the Bill of Rights, including freedom of religion and the press; guarantees of a fair trial, including the defendant's right to an impartial judge and the assistance of counsel; and the right to keep and bear arms. The Supreme Court's controversial application of the due process clause in the *Roe* v. *Wade* case led to the legalization of abortion in 1973.

The Supreme Court applied the equal protection clause of the Fourteenth Amendment in its landmark decision in *Brown* v. *Board of Education of Topeka* (1954), in which it ruled that racial segregation in public schools was unconstitutional. In the 1960s and '70s the equal protection clause was used by the Supreme Court to extend protections to other areas, including zoning laws, voting rights, and gender discrimination. The broad interpretation of this clause has also caused considerable controversy.

Twenty-seven amendments have been added to the Constitution since 1789. In addition to those mentioned earlier, other far-reaching amendments include the Sixteenth (1913), which allowed Congress to impose an income tax; the Seventeenth (1913), which provided for direct election of senators; the Nineteenth (1920), which mandated woman suffrage; and the Twenty-sixth (1971), which granted suffrage to citizens 18 years of age and older.

CHAPTER 2

The Bill of Rights

The first 10 amendments to the Constitution of the United States, adopted as a group in 1791, are known as the Bill of Rights. They are a collection of guarantees of individual rights and of limitations on federal and state governments that derived from popular dissatisfaction with the limited guarantees of the Constitution. The first Congress submitted 12 amendments (drafted by James Madison) to the states, 10 of which were ratified. The First Amendment guarantees freedom of religion, speech, and the press, and grants the right to petition for redress and to assemble peacefully. The Second Amendment guarantees the right of the people to keep and bear arms. The Third Amendment prohibits the quartering of soldiers in private dwellings in peacetime. The Fourth Amendment protects against unreasonable search and seizure. The Fifth Amendment establishes grand-jury indictment for serious offenses, protects against double jeopardy (that is, prosecuting someone more than once for the same offense) in criminal cases, and prohibits compelling testimony by a person against himself or herself. The Sixth Amendment establishes the rights of the accused to a speedy trial and an impartial jury and guarantees the right to legal counsel and to the obtaining of witnesses in his favor. The Seventh Amendment preserves the right to trial by jury in serious civil suits and prohibits double jeopardy in civil cases. The Eighth Amendment prohibits excessive bail and cruel and unusual punishment. The Ninth Amendment states that enumeration of certain rights in the Constitution does not mean the abrogation of rights not mentioned. The Tenth Amendment reserves to the states and people any powers not delegated to the federal government.

Congress of the United States,
begun and held at the City of New-York, on
Wednesday the fourth of March, one thousand seven hundred and eighty nine.

Bill of Rights of the Constitution of the United States of America. National Archives, Washington, D.C.

FIRST AMENDMENT

The First Amendment (1791) to the Constitution of the United States guarantees a number of fundamental freedoms and rights and prohibits laws that constitute an "establishment of religion." The full text of the amendment is:

> *Congress shall make no law respecting an establishment of religion, or prohibiting the free exercise thereof; or abridging the freedom of speech, or of the press; or the right of the people peaceably to assemble, and to petition the Government for a redress of grievances.*

The clauses of the amendment are often called the establishment clause, the free exercise clause, the free speech clause, the free press clause, the assembly clause, and the petition clause.

GOVERNMENT ACTIONS SUBJECT TO THE FIRST AMENDMENT

The First Amendment, like the rest of the Bill of Rights, originally restricted only what the federal government may do and did not bind the states. Most state constitutions had their own bills of rights, and those generally included provisions similar to those found in the First Amendment. But the state provisions could be enforced only by state courts.

In 1868, however, the Fourteenth Amendment was added to the U.S. Constitution, and it prohibited states from denying people "liberty" without "due process." Since then, the U.S. Supreme Court has gradually interpreted this to apply most of the Bill of Rights to state governments. In particular, from the 1920s to the '40s the Supreme Court applied all the clauses of the First Amendment to the states. Thus, the First Amendment now covers actions by the federal, state, and local governments. The First Amendment also applies to all branches of government, including legislatures, courts, juries, and executive officials and agencies. This includes public employers, public university systems, and public school systems.

The First Amendment, however, applies only to restrictions imposed by the government, since the First and Fourteenth amendments refer only to government action. As a result, if a private employer fires an employee because of the employee's speech, there is no First Amendment violation. There is likewise no violation if a private university expels a student for what the student said, if a commercial landlord restricts what bumper stickers are sold on property it owns, or if an Internet service provider refuses to host certain Web sites.

Legislatures sometimes enact laws that protect speakers or religious observers from retaliation by private organizations. For example, Title VII of the federal Civil Rights Act of 1964 bans religious discrimination even by private employers. Similarly, laws in some states prohibit employers from firing employees for off-duty political activity. But such prohibitions are imposed by legislative choice rather than by the First Amendment.

FREEDOMS OF SPEECH, PRESS, ASSEMBLY, AND PETITION

The freedoms of speech, press, assembly, and petition—discussed here together as "freedom of expression"—broadly protect expression from governmental restrictions. Thus, for instance, the government may not outlaw antiwar speech, speech praising violence, racist speech, procommunist speech, and the like. Nor may the government impose special taxes on speech on certain topics or limit demonstrations that express certain views. Furthermore, the government may not authorize civil lawsuits based on people's speech, unless the speech falls within a traditionally recognized First Amendment exception. This is why, for example, public figures may not sue for emotional distress inflicted by offensive magazine articles, unless the articles are not just offensive but include statements that fall within the "false statements of fact" exception.

The free expression guarantees are not limited to political speech. They also cover speech about science, religion, morality, and social issues as well as art and even personal gossip.

Freedom of the press confirms that the government may not restrict mass communication. It does not, however, give media businesses any additional constitutional rights beyond what nonprofessional speakers have.

Freedom of petition protects the right to communicate with government officials. This includes lobbying government officials and petitioning the courts by filing lawsuits, unless the court concludes that the lawsuit clearly lacks any legal basis.

PERMISSIBLE RESTRICTIONS ON EXPRESSION

Despite the broad freedom of expression guaranteed by the First Amendment, there are some historically rooted exceptions. First, the government may generally restrict the time, place, or manner of speech, if the restrictions are unrelated to what the speech says and leave people with enough alternative ways of expressing their views. Thus, for instance, the government may restrict the use of loudspeakers in residential neighborhoods at night, limit all demonstrations that block traffic, or ban all picketing of people's homes.

Second, a few narrow categories of speech are not protected from government restrictions. The main such categories are incitement, false statements of fact, obscenity, child pornography, fighting words, and threats. As the Supreme Court held in *Brandenburg* v. *Ohio* (1969), the government may forbid "incitement"—speech "directed at inciting or producing imminent lawless action" and "likely to incite or produce such action" (such as a speech to a mob urging it to attack a nearby building). But speech urging action at some unspecified future time may not be forbidden.

Knowing lies—such as defamation (which is called "libel" if written and "slander" if spoken), lying under oath, and fraud—may also be punished. In some instances, even negligent factual errors may lead to lawsuits. This, however, extends only to factual falsehoods; expression of opinion may not be punished even if the opinion is broadly seen as morally wrong.

Certain types of pornography, labeled obscenity by the law, may also be punished, as the Supreme Court held in *Miller* v. *California* (1973). Exactly what constitutes obscenity is not clear, but since the 1980s the definition has been quite narrow. Also, obscenities in the sense of merely vulgar words may not be punished (*Cohen* v. *California* [1971]).

Material depicting actual children engaging in sex, or being naked in a sexually suggestive context, is called child pornography and may be punished. Sexually themed material that uses adults who look like children or features hand-drawn or computer-generated pictures of fictional children does not fall within this exception, though some such material might still be punishable as obscenity.

Fighting words—defined as insults of the kind likely to provoke a physical fight—may also be punished, though general commentary on political, religious, or social matters may not be punished, even if some people are so upset by it that they want to attack the speaker. Personalized threats of illegal conduct, such as death threats, may also be punished.

No exception exists for so-called hate speech. Racist threats are unprotected by the First Amendment alongside other threats, and personally addressed racist insults might be punishable alongside other fighting words. But such speech may not be specially punished because it is racist, sexist, antigay, or hostile to some religion.

OBSCENITY

Obscenity is a legal concept used to characterize acts, utterances, writings, or illustrations that are deemed deeply offensive according to contemporary community standards of morality and decency. Although most societies have placed restrictions on the content of literary and graphic works, it was not until relatively modern times that sexuality became a major focus of societal concern. One of the first systematic efforts to suppress books deemed to be immoral or heretical was undertaken by the Roman Catholic Church in the 16th century. Modern obscenity laws can be viewed as direct responses to the social and technological changes (e.g., the creation of the printing press and the development of the Internet) that have permitted the wide and easy distribution of sexually explicit materials. The Supreme Court of the United States has ruled that materials are obscene if they appeal predominantly to a prurient (unwholesome) interest in sexual conduct, depict or describe sexual conduct in a patently offensive way, and lack serious literary, artistic, political, or scientific value. Material deemed obscene under this definition is not protected in the United States by the free speech guarantee of the First Amendment.

SPEECH ON GOVERNMENT PROPERTY AND IN GOVERNMENT-RUN INSTITUTIONS

The preceding sections have dealt with laws that apply to speakers who are using their own resources on their own property. But the government has considerable—though not unlimited—power to control speech that uses government property.

Government employees, for example, may be fired for saying things that interfere with the employer's efficiency. Elementary, junior high, and high school students may be disciplined for saying things that risk substantially disrupting the educational process or for using vulgarities at school. If the government gives people money to express the government's views, it may demand that the money not be used to express things the government does not want to support. Speech on government land or in government buildings usually may be limited, if the government does not discriminate on the basis of the viewpoint of the speech. Additionally, speech by prisoners and by members of the military may be broadly restricted.

Speech on government-owned sidewalks and in parks (often labeled "traditional public forums") is as protected against government suppression as is speech on the speaker's own property. The same is true for speech by public university students, at least when the speech is not part of class discussions or class assignments.

The government has some extra authority to restrict speech broadcast over radio and television. Because the government is considered the owner of the airwaves, it may dictate who broadcasts over the airwaves and, to some extent, what those broadcasters can say. This is why the Supreme Court, in *FCC* v. *Pacifica Foundation* (1978), upheld a ban on broadcasting vulgar words, though such words are generally constitutionally protected outside the

American comedian George Carlin (1937 – 2008), pictured here in the 1970s, was at the centre of the 1978 Supreme Court case FCC *v.* Pacifica Foundation. *His "Seven Words You Can Never Say on Television" routine led to a landmark ruling that gave the Federal Communications Commission (FCC) the right to censor radio and TV broadcasts.* Marty Temme/WireImage/Getty Images

airwaves. It is also why the Supreme Court, in *Red Lion Broadcasting Co.* v. *FCC* (1969), upheld the "fairness doctrine," which at the time required broadcasters to give time to people who wanted to present contrary viewpoints. But this extra government authority extends only to radio and television broadcasting and not to other media, including newspapers, cable television, and the Internet.

RELATED RIGHTS

The freedom of expression also protects certain kinds of conduct that are important for people to express themselves effectively. It protects a person's freedom to associate with others in groups that express messages, such as advocacy groups or political parties. It also protects those groups' freedom to exclude people whose presence may interfere with the group's speech. That was the basis for the Supreme Court's decision in *Boy Scouts of America* v. *Dale* (2000), in which the court held that the Boy Scouts, which opposes homosexuality, may exclude gay scoutmasters. The government may ban many kinds of discrimination—but not when such a ban unduly interferes with expressive groups' ability to convey their messages.

The freedom of expression likewise protects people's freedom to spend money to speak. People are thus free to buy advertisements or to print leaflets expressing their views—for instance, "Vote for Candidate X" or "Defeat Proposition Y"—and to pool money with others to express views. Corporations and unions also may spend unlimited amounts of money on political advertising as a consequence of the Supreme Court's decision in *Citizens United* v. *Federal Election Commission* (2010). But, as the court held in *Buckley* v. *Valeo* (1976), legislatures may impose dollar limits on direct contributions to political candidates because those contributions may operate as bribes and because limits on such contributions leave people free to speak independently of the candidates. The freedom of expression also protects people's right to attend criminal trials so that people can learn what is happening in order to report it to others. That applies even when the defendant, the prosecutor, and the judge prefer that the trial be closed. But the First Amendment does not ensure access to other government processes or records. Such access is usually provided by statutes, such as the federal Freedom of Information Act.

Finally, the freedom of expression protects symbolic expression, such as wearing armbands, waving flags, and burning flags. Restrictions on such behavior that are unrelated to its message—for example, fire control laws

In Boy Scouts of America v. Dale, *the U.S. Supreme Court upheld the right of the Boy Scouts to exclude gay scout leaders. As for the freedom to publicly display an opinion on the matter, the First Amendment supports the rights of Americans, such as this man, Daniel Martino, to do just that—here, in front of the Supreme Court, Apr. 26, 2000.* Alex Wong/Getty Images

banning burning anything in public or laws banning public nudity—may be constitutional. But laws that punish symbolic expression precisely because of its symbolic message are generally unconstitutional. As a result, in *Texas* v. *Johnson* (1989), the court struck down a law prohibiting the burning of the U.S. flag.

FREE EXERCISE OF RELIGION

The First Amendment's free exercise clause prohibits deliberate religious persecution and discrimination by the government. The government may not, for instance, outlaw a particular religion, refuse to hire someone from a particular religious group, or exclude the clergy from political office. Likewise, the clause prohibits the government from singling out religious practices for punishment on the basis of their religiosity. For instance, as the government allows the ordinary nonreligious killing of animals, it may not specially ban religious animal sacrifice.

The clause, however, does not limit generally applicable laws that do not single out religion. General bans on the use of marijuana or peyote, for instance, may be applied even to those who view the use of the drugs as sacramental. Similarly, religious objections do not give people a constitutional right to avoid taxes, discriminate in employment (except in the special case of religious groups discriminating in choosing their clergy), or refuse to testify in court.

Many state and federal statutes do exempt religious objectors. The military draft, for instance, has long exempted pacifists (though not those who have religious objections to some wars but not others). The prohibition of alcohol in the 1920s and early 1930s exempted sacramental wines. The federal ban on peyote and many state bans similarly exempt religious peyote users. But these exceptions exist because legislatures chose to create them—that is, the free exercise clause did not itself protect religious rights in these instances.

From 1963 to 1990 the Supreme Court took the view that the free exercise clause did require some religious exemptions from generally applicable laws. The Court acknowledged that many laws had to be applied to everyone, including to religious objectors (e.g., laws against murder or trespassing). But the Court held that such religious exemptions could be denied only if denying them was necessary to accomplish a very important government goal. This rule became known as the Sherbert/Yoder test, named for the Court's rulings in *Sherbert* v. *Verner* (1963) and *Wisconsin* v. *Yoder* (1972), in which the Court strongly enforced this religious exemption requirement.

In practice, however, even from 1963 to 1990, religious exemptions were rarely granted. Courts routinely concluded that denying such exemptions was indeed necessary to accomplish various important goals. Finally, in 1990, in *Employment Division* v. *Smith*, the Supreme Court generally rejected the Sherbert/Yoder test, holding that the free exercise clause does not require legislatures to grant religious exemptions.

In response, more than a dozen state legislatures enacted general statutes—often called "Religious Freedom Restoration Acts"—that authorize courts to create religious exemptions from state and local government actions, using the Sherbert/Yoder test. Congress passed a similar statute that applies to federal government actions. Courts in another dozen states have interpreted their state constitutions' religious freedom provisions as requiring the Sherbert/Yoder test. But, like other religious exemptions, these rules are chosen by legislatures (or state courts) and are therefore not required by the federal free exercise clause.

THE ESTABLISHMENT CLAUSE

The framers of the Constitution were familiar with the English "established church"—that is, an official church that received extensive government support, whose leaders were entitled to seats in Parliament, and whose members had legal rights that members of other denominations lacked. The establishment clause prevented the establishment of a national church. Now that the First Amendment has been applied to the states, it also prevents the establishment of state churches. (Such was the case with the previously mentioned Congregationalism, which, up until the 1830s, was the official state-supported religion of Massachusetts.)

There is enduring controversy, however, about what the ban on the "establishment of religion" means with regard to other, more modest church-state interactions. The Supreme Court has sometimes said that the clause requires a "separation of church and state," a characterization used by Thomas Jefferson. But this still leaves unclear exactly what "separation" means.

Some legal rules in this area are well-settled and uncontroversial. For example, the government may not pressure people to participate in a religious practice (e.g., prayer), and it may not discriminate between religious groups. The government also may not decide theological questions; for instance, a state law may not provide that when a church splits, the property will go to the faction that most closely follows the church's traditional theology.

The clause also generally prohibits any special burdens imposed on people who are not religious or special benefits given to religious people. There is an important exception, however: the government may sometimes choose to exempt religious objectors from generally applicable laws without similarly exempting nonreligious objectors. Thus, for instance, a federal law requires that prison inmates' religious practices (e.g., special religious diets) be accommodated, when such accommodations are consistent with prison security. The Supreme Court has held that this is constitutional, even though the law is limited to religious practices.

The establishment clause does not prohibit voters from enacting laws based on their religious beliefs, if those laws deal with nonreligious subjects. Religious people are as entitled as nonreligious people to enact their moral views into law—for instance, with regard to civil rights, alcohol use, the environment, abortion, or sexual practices. If those laws are struck down, as, for example, many abortion laws have been, this would be under other constitutional principles—such as the right to privacy—that apply regardless of whether the laws are motivated by religious beliefs.

Beyond these relatively uncontroversial principles lie areas where the Supreme Court has long been divided, often by a 5-to-4 margin. The current official rule, set forth in *Lemon* v. *Kurtzman* (1971), holds that government actions violate the establishment clause if they have a primarily religious purpose, have a primary effect either of advancing or of inhibiting religion, or excessively entangle the government in religious matters. This test, however, is both controversial and vague. By itself, it gives little guidance about, for example, what constitutes "excessive entanglement" or which of a law's many effects should be considered "primary."

Any clarity in understanding what the establishment clause allows or prohibits comes from the other rules that the Supreme Court has created, sometimes using the Lemon test. First, the government may not communicate in ways that a reasonable observer would see as endorsing religion, such as by putting up stand-alone nativity scenes in celebration of Christmas or posting displays focused on the Ten Commandments. But religious symbols may be placed alongside nonreligious symbols in broader displays, such as in museum exhibitions or displays celebrating the winter holidays generally.

The government may also sometimes engage in religious speech when the practice is deeply historically rooted. This exception for long-standing practices has been applied, for example, to uphold prayers given by government-paid legislative chaplains. Some originally religious speech—such as naming cities "Corpus Christi" or "Providence" or using "In God We Trust" on currency—is likewise seen as constitutionally permissible because it now has nonreligious or historical significance beyond its purely religious meaning.

Second, government programs are unconstitutional if they are intended to promote religion. It is on this basis that the Supreme Court has struck down state restrictions on the teaching of evolution in public schools and state requirements that public schools teach creationism alongside evolution.

Third, the government is limited in providing benefits to religious institutions, including religious schools, even when those benefits come through evenhanded government programs open equally to secular and religious institutions. In the 1970s and '80s this restriction was interpreted broadly, effectively requiring the government to exclude religious institutions from most such programs.

Since the 1990s the restriction has been narrowed. First, if an evenhanded government program gives funding to individual recipients, those individuals may use the funding at religious institutions as well as at nonreligious ones. A classic example of this in action is the G.I. Bill—passed following World War II—which paid for veterans to go to any college of their choice. By analogy to the G.I. Bill, the Supreme Court's decision in *Zelman* v. *Simmons-Harris* (2002) upheld school voucher programs that fund parents' choices to send their children to public, private nonreligious, or private religious schools.

Second, even if the program in question gives funds or benefits directly to the institutions rather than to individuals, religious institutions are able to participate if they ensure that the funds or benefits are not used for religious purposes. The federal government, for instance, may lend computer equipment to a wide range of schools, if the schools do not use the equipment to teach religious topics.

SECOND AMENDMENT

The Second Amendment to the Constitution of the United States (1791) provides a constitutional check on congressional power under Article I Section 8 to organize, arm, and discipline the federal militia. The full text of the amendment is:

> *A well regulated Militia, being necessary to the security of a free State, the right of the people to keep and bear Arms, shall not be infringed.*

The Second Amendment was envisioned by the framers of the Constitution, according to College of William and Mary law professor and future U.S. District Court judge St. George Tucker in 1803 in his great work *Blackstone's Commentaries: With Notes of Reference to the Constitution and Laws of the Federal Government of the United States and of the Commonwealth of Virginia*, as the "true palladium of liberty." In addition to checking federal power, the Second Amendment also provided state governments with what

Luther Martin (1744/48–1826) described as the "last coup de grace" that would enable the states "to thwart and oppose the general government." Last, it enshrined the ancient Florentine and Roman constitutional principle of civil and military virtue by making every citizen a soldier and every soldier a citizen.

SUPREME COURT INTERPRETATIONS

Until 2008 the Supreme Court of the United States had never seriously considered the constitutional scope of the Second Amendment. In its first hearing on the subject, in *Presser* v. *Illinois* (1886), the Supreme Court held that the Second Amendment prevented the states from "prohibit[ing] the people from keeping and bearing arms, so as to deprive the United States of their rightful resource for maintaining the public security." More than four decades later, in *United States* v. *Schwimmer* (1929), the Supreme Court cited the Second Amendment as enshrining that the duty of individuals "to defend our government against all enemies whenever necessity arises is a fundamental principle of the Constitution" and holding that "the common defense was one of the purposes for which the people ordained and established the Constitution." Meanwhile, in *United States* v. *Miller* (1939), in a prosecution under the National Firearms Act (1934), the Supreme Court avoided addressing the constitutional scope of the Second Amendment by merely holding that the "possession or use of a shotgun having a barrel of less than eighteen inches in length" was not "any part of the ordinary military equipment" protected by the Second Amendment.

For more than seven decades after the *United States* v. *Miller* decision, what right to bear arms that the Second Amendment protected remained uncertain. This uncertainty was ended, however, in *District of Columbia* v. *Heller*

(2008), in which the Supreme Court examined the Second Amendment in exacting detail. In a narrow 5–4 majority, delivered by Antonin Scalia, the Supreme Court held that self-defense was the "central component" of the amendment and that the District of Columbia's "prohibition against rendering any lawful firearm in the home operable for the purpose of immediate self-defense" was unconstitutional. The Supreme Court also affirmed previous rulings that the Second Amendment ensured the right of individuals to take part in the defense of their liberties by taking up arms in an organized militia. However, the Court was clear to emphasize that the "organized militia" is not "the sole institutional beneficiary of the Second Amendment's guarantee."

Because the *Heller* ruling constrained only federal regulations against the right of armed self-defense in the home, it was unclear whether the Court would hold that the Second Amendment guarantees established in *Heller* were equally applicable to the states. The Supreme Court answered this question in 2010, with its ruling on *McDonald* v. *Chicago*. In a plurality opinion, a 5–4 majority held that the *Heller* "right to possess a handgun in the home for the purpose of self-defense" is applicable to the states through the Fourteenth Amendment's due process clause.

However, despite the use of "person" in the Fourteenth Amendment's due process clause, the *McDonald* plurality opinion did not extend to noncitizens. Clarence Thomas's fifth and decisive vote extended the Second Amendment right recognized in *Heller* only to citizens. Thomas wrote, "Because this case does not involve a claim brought by a noncitizen, I express no view on the difference, if any, between my conclusion and the plurality with respect to the extent to which States may regulate firearm possession by noncitizens." Thomas further came to this conclusion because he thought the Second Amendment should be incorporated through the Fourteenth Amendment's "privileges or immunities" clause, which recognizes only the rights of "citizens."

The relatively narrow holdings in the *McDonald* and *Heller* decisions left many Second Amendment legal issues unsettled, including the constitutionality of many federal gun control regulations, whether the right to carry or conceal a weapon in public was protected, and whether noncitizens are protected through the equal protection clause.

ORIGINS AND HISTORICAL ANTECEDENTS

The origins of the Second Amendment can be traced to ancient Roman and Florentine times, but its English origins lie in the late 16th century, when Queen Elizabeth I attempted to institute a national militia in which individuals of all classes would be required by law to take part. Although her attempt failed miserably, the ideology of the militia would be used as a political tool up to the mid-18th century. The political debate over the establishment and control of the militia was a contributing factor in both the English Civil Wars (1642–51) and the Glorious Revolution (1688–89).

Despite recognition in the early 21st century by the Supreme Court that the Second Amendment protected armed individual self-defense in the home, many constitutional historians disagreed with the Court that the Second Amendment protected anything but the right to participate in a militia force as the means of defending their liberties. For more than two centuries there was a consensus that the Second Amendment protected only the right of individuals to "keep and bear Arms" in order to take part in defending their liberties as a militia force.

However, by the late 20th century the popular consensus had shifted, many believing that the Second Amendment was framed to protect armed self-defense in the home.

In England, following the Glorious Revolution, the Second Amendment's predecessor was codified in the British Bill of Rights in 1689, under its Article VII, which proclaimed "that the subjects which are Protestants may have arms for their defence suitable to their conditions and as allowed by law." Often misinterpreted as a right to defend one's person, home, or property, the allowance to "have arms" ensured that Parliament could exercise its sovereign right of self-preservation against a tyrannical crown by arming qualified Protestants as a militia.

The framers of the U.S. Constitution undoubtedly had in mind the English allowance to "have arms" when drafting the Second Amendment. The constitutional significance of a "well regulated Militia" is well documented in English and American history from the late 17th century through the American Revolution; it was included in the Articles of Confederation (1781), the country's first constitution, and was even noted at the Constitutional Convention that drafted the new U.S. Constitution in Philadelphia in 1787. The right to "keep and bear Arms" was thus included as a means to accomplish the objective of a "well regulated Militia"—to provide for the defense of the nation, to provide a well-trained and disciplined force to check federal tyranny, and to bring constitutional balance by distributing the power of the sword equally among the people, the states, and the federal government.

THIRD AMENDMENT

The Third Amendment (1791) to the Constitution of the United States prohibits the involuntary quartering of soldiers in private homes. The full text of the amendment is:

No Soldier shall, in time of peace be quartered in any house, without the consent of the Owner, nor in time of war, but in a manner to be prescribed by law.

Although the Third Amendment has never been the direct subject of Supreme Court scrutiny, its core principles were among the most salient at the time of the founding of the republic. Prior to and during the American Revolution, the British, under King George III, maintained what amounted to standing armies in the colonies, with soldiers commonly quartered in private homes. This constant military presence and the abuses to individuals and property associated with it not only galvanized colonial opposition to the British but also compelled Thomas Jefferson to specifically admonish King George III in the Declaration of Independence "for quartering large bodies of armed troops among us." With the conclusion of the Revolution and the ratification of the Constitution, support for an amendment that would prohibit the quartering of troops in times of peace was a paramount concern. However, as the history of the country progressed with little conflict on American soil, the amendment has had little occasion to be invoked. As a matter of constitutional law, it has become one marginally cited piece of the fabric of privacy rights jurisprudence.

FOURTH AMENDMENT

The Fourth Amendment (1791) to the Constitution of the United States forbids unreasonable searches and seizures of individuals and property. The full text of the amendment is:

The right of the people to be secure in their persons, houses, papers, and effects, against unreasonable searches and seizures, shall not be violated, and no Warrants shall issue, but upon probable cause, supported by Oath or affirmation, and particularly describing the place to be searched, and the persons or things to be seized.

Introduced in 1789, what became the Fourth Amendment struck at the heart of a matter central to the early American experience: the principle that, within reason, "Every man's house is his castle," and that any citizen may fall into the category of the criminally accused and ought to be provided protections accordingly. In U.S. constitutional law, the Fourth Amendment is the foundation of criminal law jurisprudence, articulating both the rights of persons and the responsibilities of law enforcement officials. The balance between these two forces has undergone considerable public, political, and judicial debate. Are the amendment's two clauses meant to be applied independently or taken as a whole? Is the expectation of privacy diminished depending on where and what is suspected, sought, and seized? What constitutes an "unreasonable" search and seizure?

The protections contained in the amendment have been determined less on the basis of what the Constitution says than according to what it has been interpreted to mean, and, as such, its constitutional meaning has inherently been fluid. The protections granted by the U.S. Supreme Court have expanded during periods when the Court was dominated by liberals (e.g., during the tenure of Chief Justice Earl Warren [1953–69]), beginning particularly with *Mapp* v. *Ohio* (1961), in which the Court extended the exclusionary rule to all criminal proceedings; by contrast, during the tenure of the conservative William Rehnquist (1986–2005) as chief justice, the Court contracted the rights afforded to the criminally accused, allowing law enforcement officials latitude to search in instances when they reasonably believed that the property in question harboured presumably dangerous persons.

FIFTH AMENDMENT

The Fifth Amendment (1791) to the Constitution of the United States articulates procedural safeguards designed to protect the rights of the criminally accused and to secure life, liberty, and property. The full text of the amendment is:

> *No person shall be held to answer for a capital, or otherwise infamous crime, unless on a presentment or indictment of a Grand Jury, except in cases arising in the land or naval forces, or in the Militia, when in actual service in time of War or public danger; nor shall any person be subject for the same offence to be twice put in jeopardy of life or limb; nor shall be compelled in any criminal case to be a witness against himself, nor be deprived of life, liberty, or property, without due process of law; nor shall private property be taken for public use without just compensation.*

GRAND JURIES

Similar to the First Amendment, the Fifth Amendment is divided into five clauses, representing five distinct yet related rights. The first clause specifies that "[n]o person shall be held to answer for a capital, or otherwise infamous crime, unless on a presentment or indictment of a Grand Jury, except in cases arising in the land or naval forces or in the Militia, when in actual service in time of War or public danger." This "grand jury" provision requires a body to make a formal "presentment" or "indictment" of a person accused of committing a crime against the laws of the federal government. The proceeding is not a trial but rather an ex parte hearing (i.e., one in which only one party, the prosecution, presents evidence) to determine if the government has enough evidence to carry a case to trial. If the grand jury finds sufficient evidence that an offense was committed, it issues an indictment, which then permits a trial. The portion of the clause pertaining to exceptions in cases "arising in the land or naval forces, or in the Militia" is a corollary to Article I, Section 8, which grants Congress the power "[t]o make Rules for the Government and Regulation of the land and naval Forces." Combined, they justify the use of military courts for the armed forces, thus denying military personnel the same procedural rights afforded civilians.

DOUBLE JEOPARDY

The second section is commonly referred to as the "double jeopardy" clause, and it protects citizens against a second prosecution after an acquittal or a conviction, as well as against multiple punishments for the same offense. This provision does not preclude prosecutions for both civil and criminal aspects of an offense or for conspiracy to commit as well as committing an offense. Nor does it prohibit separate trials for acts that violate laws of both the federal and state governments, although federal laws generally suppress prosecution by the national government if a person is convicted of the same crime in a state proceeding.

SELF-INCRIMINATION

The third section is commonly referred to as the "self-incrimination" clause, and it protects persons accused of committing a crime from being forced to testify against themselves. In the U.S. judicial system a person is presumed innocent, and it is the responsibility of the state (or national government) to prove guilt. Like other pieces of evidence, once presented, words can be used powerfully against a person; however, words can be manipulated in a way that many other objects cannot. Consequently, information gained from sobriety tests, police lineups, voice samples, and the like is constitutionally permissible while evidence gained from compelled testimony is not. As such, persons accused of committing crimes are protected against themselves or, more accurately, how their words may be used against them. The clause, therefore, protects a key aspect of "the system" as well as the rights of the criminally accused.

DUE PROCESS

The fourth section is commonly referred to as the "due process" clause. It protects life, liberty, and property from impairment by the federal government. (The Fourteenth Amendment, ratified in 1868, protects the same rights from infringement by the states.) Chiefly concerned with fairness and justice, the due process clause seeks to preserve and protect fundamental rights and ensure that any deprivation of life, liberty, or property occurs in accordance with procedural safeguards. As such, there are both substantive and procedural considerations associated with the due process clause, and this has influenced the development of two separate tracks of due process jurisprudence: procedural and substantive. Procedural due process pertains to the rules, elements, or methods of enforcement—that is, its procedural aspects. Thus, with respect to the elements of a fair trial and related Sixth Amendment protections, as long as all relevant rights of the accused are adequately protected—as long as the rules of the game, so to speak, are followed—then the government may, in fact, deprive a person of his or her life, liberty, or property. But what if the rules are not fair? What if the law itself—regardless of how it is enforced—seemingly deprives rights? This raises the controversial spectre of substantive due process rights. It is not inconceivable that the content of the law, regardless of how it is enforced, is itself repugnant to the Constitution because it violates fundamental rights. Over time, the Supreme Court has had an on-again, off-again relationship with liberty-based due process challenges, but it has generally abided by the principle that certain rights are "implicit in the concept of ordered liberty" (*Palko* v. *Connecticut* [1937]), and as such they are afforded constitutional protection. This, in turn, has led to the expansion of the meaning of the term *liberty*. What arguably began as "freedom from restraint" has been transformed into a virtual cornucopia of rights reasonably related to enumerated rights, without which neither liberty nor justice would exist. For example, the right to an abortion, established in *Roe* v. *Wade* (1973), grew from privacy rights, which emerged from the penumbras (implied rights) of the Constitution.

TAKINGS

The Fifth Amendment mentions property twice—once in the due process clause and again as the amendment's entire final clause, commonly known as the "takings clause." The common denominator of property rights is the concept of fairness that applies to the authority of the federal government to acquire private property. At the time of ratification, property determined wealth and status. It entitled a person to participate in politics and government. It was cherished and keenly protected.

Despite this, it was understood that individual rights must sometimes yield to societal rights and that representative governments must accordingly provide the greatest good for the greatest number. The growth and development of the United States ultimately would bring challenges to existing property lines, and it was necessary for an amendment to provide rules governing the acquisition of property. As such, the takings clause empowers the government to exercise eminent domain in order to take private property; however, such takings must be for public use and provide adequate compensation to landowners. Throughout most of American history this balance of individual and societal rights hinged on the government's fidelity to the cornerstone principles of public use and just compensation, and in many respects it still does. However, in 2005 *Kelo* v. *City of New London* brought a new twist to takings clause jurisprudence. Whereas prior to the *Kelo* ruling, the government would acquire property for public use directly, in the *Kelo* case the Supreme Court upheld the use of eminent domain to take private property for commercial development that was assumed to indirectly provide a positive impact for the public.

SIXTH AMENDMENT

The Sixth Amendment (1791) to the Constitution of the United States effectively established the procedures governing criminal courts. The full text of the amendment is:

> *In all criminal prosecutions, the accused shall enjoy the right to a speedy and public trial, by an impartial jury of the State and district wherein the crime shall have been committed, which district shall have been previously ascertained by law, and to be informed of the nature and cause of the accusation;*

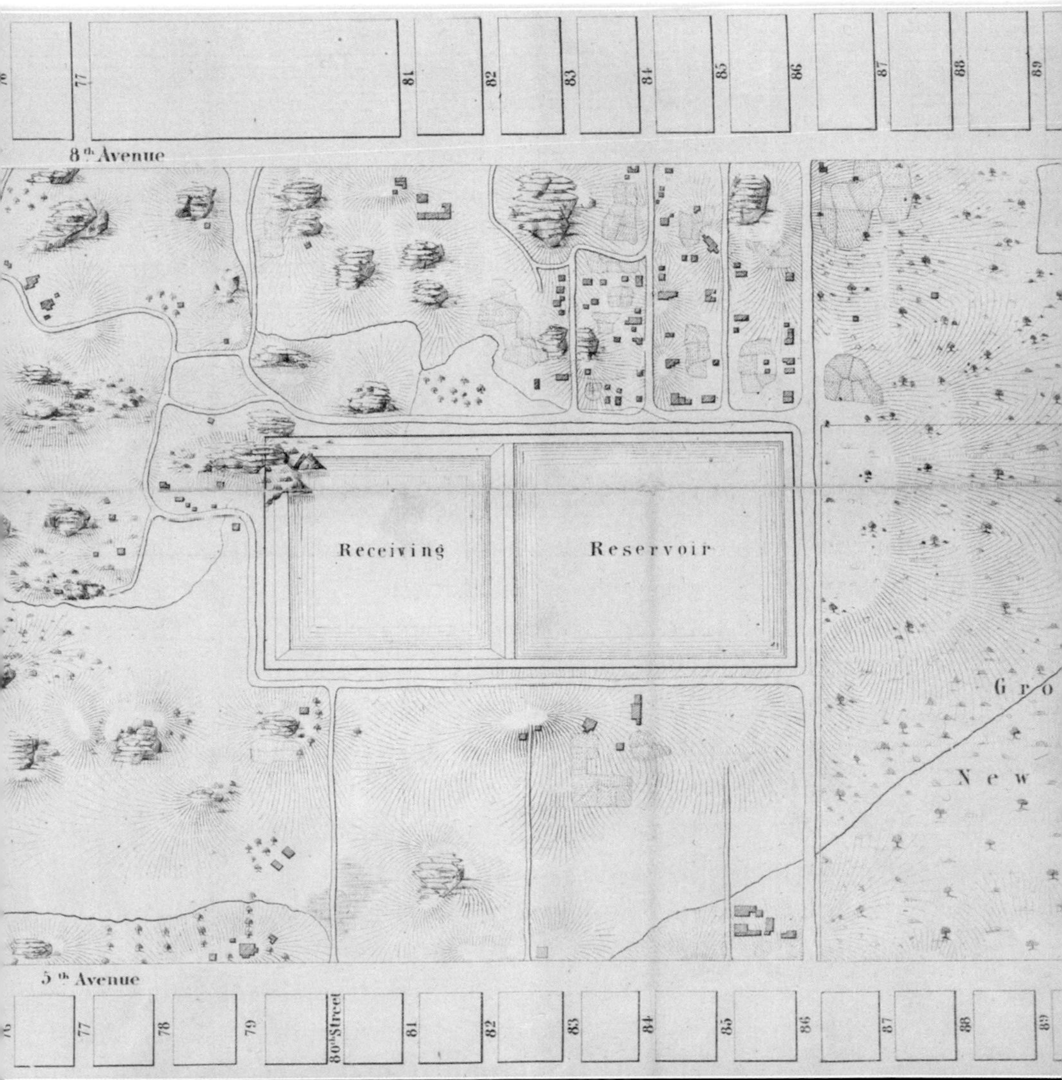

Seneca Village, a 19th-century village of predominantly African-American property owners, sat on what was to become part of Central Park. The village, which was located along the western edge of where the park is now situated, included 60 homes, 3 churches, several cemeteries, and a grade school. First settled in 1825 by freed blacks, Seneca Village was razed in 1857, its over 250 inhabitants evicted from their homes on the basis of eminent domain, the power of the state to take private property for public use. This topographical map, drawn in 1856 by engineer Egbert Viele, shows the village prior to its destruction. Collection of the New-York Historical Society, Neg. No. 67835

to be confronted with the witnesses against him; to have compulsory process for obtaining Witnesses in his favor, and to have the assistance of counsel for his defence.

Based on the principle that justice delayed is justice denied, the amendment balances societal and individual rights in its first clause by requiring a "speedy" trial. It also satisfies the democratic expectation of transparency and fairness in criminal law by requiring public trials consisting of impartial jurors.

The public trial and jury requirements contained in the Sixth Amendment's first clause are essential elements of due process. An integral part of the clause and the rights it seeks to protect is impartiality. Bias is expected to be reduced not only by placing decision making in the hands of jurors but also by screening out potentially prejudiced jurors. To this end, both the prosecution and the defense have the opportunity to participate in the jury selection process.

Transparency and fairness in criminal law are also evident in the accusation and confrontation clauses of the amendment. Criminal suspects must be made aware of the crimes they are accused of committing, and this comes mostly in the form of an indictment, a precise and detailed list of charges for which the criminally accused will be tried. The confrontation clause reinforces the rights of the criminally accused further by requiring that they be confronted with the witnesses against them. In addition to providing defendants the opportunity to see their accusers, the clause serves the vital role of having the witnesses available for cross-examination. Moreover, defendants are entitled to witnesses in their defense. Any person knowledgeable of the facts of a case may be called as a witness for the defense.

The Sixth Amendment's final clause entitles the criminally accused to legal counsel and applies equally to custodial interrogations and trials. In either environment, absent legal assistance the criminally accused may be intimidated or compelled to provide testimony against his or her will. Absent the specialized knowledge of the law and criminal procedure, the accused would not be able to mount an effective defense of his or her own liberty. Thus, without the right to legal counsel, the criminal justice system would be lopsided in favour of the government, and this right to counsel enables the playing field to be leveled.

SEVENTH AMENDMENT

The Seventh Amendment (1791) to the Constitution of the United States formally established the rules governing civil trials. The full text of the amendment is:

> *In Suits at common law, where the value in controversy shall exceed twenty dollars, the right of trial by jury shall be preserved, and no fact tried by a jury, shall be otherwise reexamined in any Court of the United States, than according to the rules of the common law.*

The amendment's objective was to preserve a distinction between the responsibilities of the courts (such as deciding matters of law) and those of juries (such as deciding matters of fact).

Many of the Seventh Amendment's provisions were rooted in the English common-law tradition, and over time they have experienced only marginal change. While the number of jurors has been reduced from 12 (which was the common-law norm) to 6, and while parties may waive their right to trial by jury in favour of a direct verdict, other distinguishing characteristics of the common-law tradition (such as the unanimous verdict requirement) and the amendment (the financial threshold) remain intact. The Seventh Amendment is an unincorporated right, meaning that it has not been brought under the scope of protection offered to the states under the Fourteenth Amendment's due process clause.

EIGHTH AMENDMENT

The Eighth Amendment (1791) to the Constitution of the United States limits the sanctions that may be imposed by the criminal justice system on those accused or convicted of criminal behavior. The full text of the amendment is:

> *Excessive bail shall not be required, nor excessive fines imposed, nor cruel and unusual punishments inflicted.*

The three clauses of the amendment restrict the amount of bail associated with a criminal infraction, the fines that may be imposed, and the punishments that may be inflicted. The Eighth Amendment comes almost verbatim (word for word) from the English Bill of Rights (1689), which states: "That excessive bail ought not to be required, nor excessive fines imposed, nor cruel and unusual punishments inflicted."

While the U.S. Constitution is silent on what constitutes "excessive" bail or fines, the general rule has been to allow fines that do not violate due process by resulting in a loss of property. Absent an apparent abuse of discretion in imposing fines, appeals to fines are not generally reversed. With regard to bail, individual rights are tempered by the interests of the legal system and society at large. Thus, the seriousness of the crime, the evidence against the accused, and the flight risk of the accused may be taken into consideration when determining amounts. Reasonableness and proportionality are generally taken into account when fixing bail amounts for criminal infractions.

The Constitution is likewise silent on what kinds of punishment are "cruel" and "unusual," and it has been left for the courts to determine precisely what is and what is not permissible under the law. The undergirding principle is that the punishment should be proportional to the crime. Is capital punishment permissible? May a teenager be sentenced to death? May a juvenile be sentenced to life in prison without the possibility of parole? Should someone with a mental disability be subject to the death penalty? These are but a few of the questions that the Supreme Court has been asked to consider. Because of the subjective nature of what constitutes a cruel or unusual punishment and the clear, direct, and tangible losses of liberty and even life associated with it, challenges to statutes on Eighth Amendment grounds are plentiful, and the ideological complexion of the Supreme Court has influenced what it will or will not permit.

When the Eighth Amendment was ratified in the late 18th century, it was understood that barbaric punishments and those wholly disproportionate to the crime or to societal tolerance would be prohibited. Still, what was acceptable in late 18th-century America was not necessarily so in subsequent periods. In 1791, for example, larceny, burglary, and even forgery could in some cases result in hanging. Less than a century later, however, in *Whitten* v. *Georgia* (1872), the Supreme Court put limits on what was constitutionally permissible, holding that the "cruel and unusual" clause was "intended to prohibit the barbarities of quartering, hanging in chains, castration, etc." Similarly, in *In re Kemmler* (1890), when the electric chair was introduced as a humane method of execution, the Supreme

Court held it constitutional because death was "instantaneous" and "painless," unlike the lingering deaths that resulted from "burning at the stake, crucifixion, breaking on the wheel, or the like."

In general, the Supreme Court has held that the "due process" clauses of the Fifth and Fourteenth amendments generally allow that a convicted defendant's life may be taken as long as the defendant's rights are not sacrificed. Whether or not capital punishment itself could constitute a cruel and unusual punishment was tested in the 1970s. In a 5–4 ruling in *Furman* v. *Georgia* (1972), the Supreme

Pictured in 2007 at the Texas Prison Museum in Huntsville, TX, this decommissioned electric chair electrocuted 361 prisoners between 1924 and 1964. The chair, made by prison workers, garnered the rather ghoulish nickname of "Old Sparky," a moniker given to many such chairs across the United States. Over the course of the 20th and early-21st centuries, court challenges regarding the cruel and unusual nature of electrocution led most states to abandon the practice in favour of lethal injection. AFP/ Getty Images

Court consolidated three cases, one (*Furman*) in which a gun accidentally went off while the defendant was burglarizing a home and two (*Jackson* v. *Georgia* and *Branch* v. *Texas*) in which the death penalty for rape was challenged. The Supreme Court held that the death sentences imposed in these three cases violated the Constitution because they provided too much discretion in meting out death sentences; it further stipulated that the imposition of the death penalty in general had been "arbitrary" and "capricious" and thus invalidated capital punishment until states could redress this. Over the next several years, state legislatures enacted different methods that they hoped would pass constitutional muster; by 1976 one method, so-called guided discretion, was held constitutional by the Supreme Court, but a second, mandatory capital punishment, was deemed unconstitutional.

NINTH AMENDMENT

The Ninth Amendment (1791) to the Constitution of the United States provides that the people retain rights absent specific enumeration. The full text of the amendment is:

> *The enumeration in the Constitution, of certain rights, shall not be construed to deny or disparage others retained by the people.*

Prior to, during, and after ratification of the Constitution, debate raged about the protection of individual rights. Initially, the Constitution contained no Bill of Rights, but one was added at the urging of the Anti-Federalists, who feared that without it too much power would be vested in the federal government. Federalists, who believed that the Constitution had created a limited central government countered that an enumeration of protected rights could be a detriment to individual liberties by implying that other liberties were unworthy of constitutional protection. Thus was born the Ninth Amendment, whose purpose was to assert the principle that the enumerated rights are not exhaustive and final and that the listing of certain rights does not deny or disparage the existence of other rights. What rights were protected by the amendment was left unclear.

Since the enactment of the Bill of Rights, the U.S. Supreme Court has never relied solely (or primarily) on the Ninth Amendment, and through the mid-1960s it was mentioned only sparingly. Indeed, in 1955 in a lecture (later turned into book form) titled "The Supreme Court in the American System of Government," Associate Justice Robert H. Jackson admitted that the Ninth Amendment was a "mystery" to him. Since that time, however, the Ninth Amendment has been used as a secondary source of liberties and has emerged as important in the extension of rights to protect privacy.

In 1965 in *Griswold* v. *State of Connecticut*, the Supreme Court held that married couples had the right to use birth control. The majority decision rested on Fourth and Fifth amendment grounds, but Associate Justice Arthur Goldberg in his concurring opinion argued squarely on Ninth Amendment principles, stating:

> *The language and history of the Ninth Amendment reveal that the Framers of the Constitution believed that there are additional fundamental rights, protected from governmental infringement, which exist alongside those fundamental rights specifically mentioned in the first eight constitutional amendments.*

Taking that argument one step further, Goldberg claimed that:

> *other fundamental personal rights should not be denied such protection or disparaged in any other way simply because they are not specifically listed in the first eight constitutional amendments.*

Goldberg's invoking of the Ninth Amendment was criticized by Hugo L. Black and Potter Stewart in their dissent, since the constitutional provision does not define which rights are retained by the people. They wrote that:

> *to say that the Ninth Amendment has anything to do with this case is to turn somersaults with history....Until today, no member of this Court has ever suggested that the Ninth Amendment meant anything else, and the idea that a federal court could ever use the Ninth Amendment to annul a law passed by the elected representatives of the people of the State of Connecticut would have caused James Madison no little wonder.*

In the decades since the *Griswold* decision, numerous claims were made in federal filings that additional rights were protected by the Ninth Amendment (almost all were rejected), and there has been considerable debate as to what protections, if any, are guaranteed by it. Some federal courts have used the Ninth Amendment as a guidepost in their decisions, but it still has not been central to any decision.

TENTH AMENDMENT

The Tenth Amendment (1791) to the Constitution of the United States formally recognizes the "reserved" powers of the states. The full text of the amendment is:

The powers not delegated to the United States by the Constitution, nor prohibited by it to the States, are reserved to the States respectively, or to the people.

The final of the 10 amendments that constitute the Bill of Rights, the Tenth Amendment was inserted into the Constitution largely to relieve tension and assuage the fears that existed among states' rights advocates who believed that the newly adopted Constitution would enable the federal government to run roughshod over the states and their citizens. While the Federalists, who advocated for a strong central government, prevailed with the ratification of the Constitution, it was essential to the integrity of the document and the stability of the fledgling country to acknowledge the interests of the Anti-Federalists, such as Patrick Henry, who unsuccessfully opposed the strong central government envisioned in the Constitution.

Whereas the Ninth Amendment states that those rights enumerated in the Constitution do not disparage other unenumerated rights retained by the people, the Tenth Amendment clearly indicates that the states are entitled to the rights not delegated to the federal government. The Tenth Amendment does not impose any specific limitations on the authority of the federal government; though there had been an attempt to do so, Congress defeated a motion to modify the word *delegated* with *expressly* in the amendment. It thus does not grant states additional powers, nor does it alter the relationship that exists between the federal government and the states. It merely indicates that the states may establish and maintain their own laws and policies so long as they do not conflict with the authority of the federal government.

In a test of the Constitution's "necessary and proper" clause (found in Article I) against the Tenth

Amendment, in *McCulloch* v. *Maryland* (1819), Chief Justice John Marshall wrote in the Supreme Court's opinion that the federal government was not prohibited from exercising only those powers specifically granted to it by the Constitution:

> *Even the 10th Amendment, which was framed for the purpose of quieting the excessive jealousies which had been excited, omits the word "expressly," and declares only that the powers "not delegated to the United States, nor prohibited to the States, are reserved to the States or to the people," thus leaving the question whether the particular power which may become the subject of contest has been delegated to the one Government, or prohibited to the other, to depend on a fair construction of the whole instrument. The men who drew and adopted this amendment had experienced the embarrassments resulting from the insertion of this word in the Articles of Confederation, and probably omitted it to avoid those embarrassments.*

However, from the death of Marshall until the 1930s and again from the mid-1980s, the U.S. Supreme Court often used the Tenth Amendment to limit the authority of the federal government, particularly with regard to regulating commerce and with regard to taxation, though it generally stood firm on the supremacy of the national government and the U.S. Constitution. In contemporary political debate, conservatives often point to the Tenth Amendment as a means of arguing in favour of restrictions on federal authority.

CHAPTER 3

The Eleventh through Twenty-seventh Amendments

Following the ratification of the Bill of Rights in 1791, 17 additional amendments to the U.S. Constitution were adopted over the course of nearly 200 years (1791–1992). Among all amendments, the Twenty-seventh (1992) took the longest time to ratify, more than 200 years, while the Twenty-sixth (1971) took the shortest time, slightly more than three months. The Twenty-first (1933), which removed the federal prohibition of alcohol imposed by the Eighteenth (1919), is the only amendment whose main purpose was to repeal another amendment; the Eighteenth, by the same token, is the only amendment to have been repealed.

ELEVENTH AMENDMENT

The Eleventh Amendment (1795) to the Constitution of the United States established the principle of state sovereign immunity. Under the authority of the amendment, the states are shielded from suits brought by citizens of other states or foreign countries. The Eleventh Amendment was, for all intents and purposes, the first amendment designed to correct, or at least to clarify, a seemingly straightforward and unproblematic element of the Constitution. In Article III, Section 2, the federal judiciary is given authority to decide "Controversies...between a State and Citizens of another State." Although it was presumed (wrongly) that the doctrine of sovereign immunity was clearly understood to preclude such actions, the U.S. Supreme Court

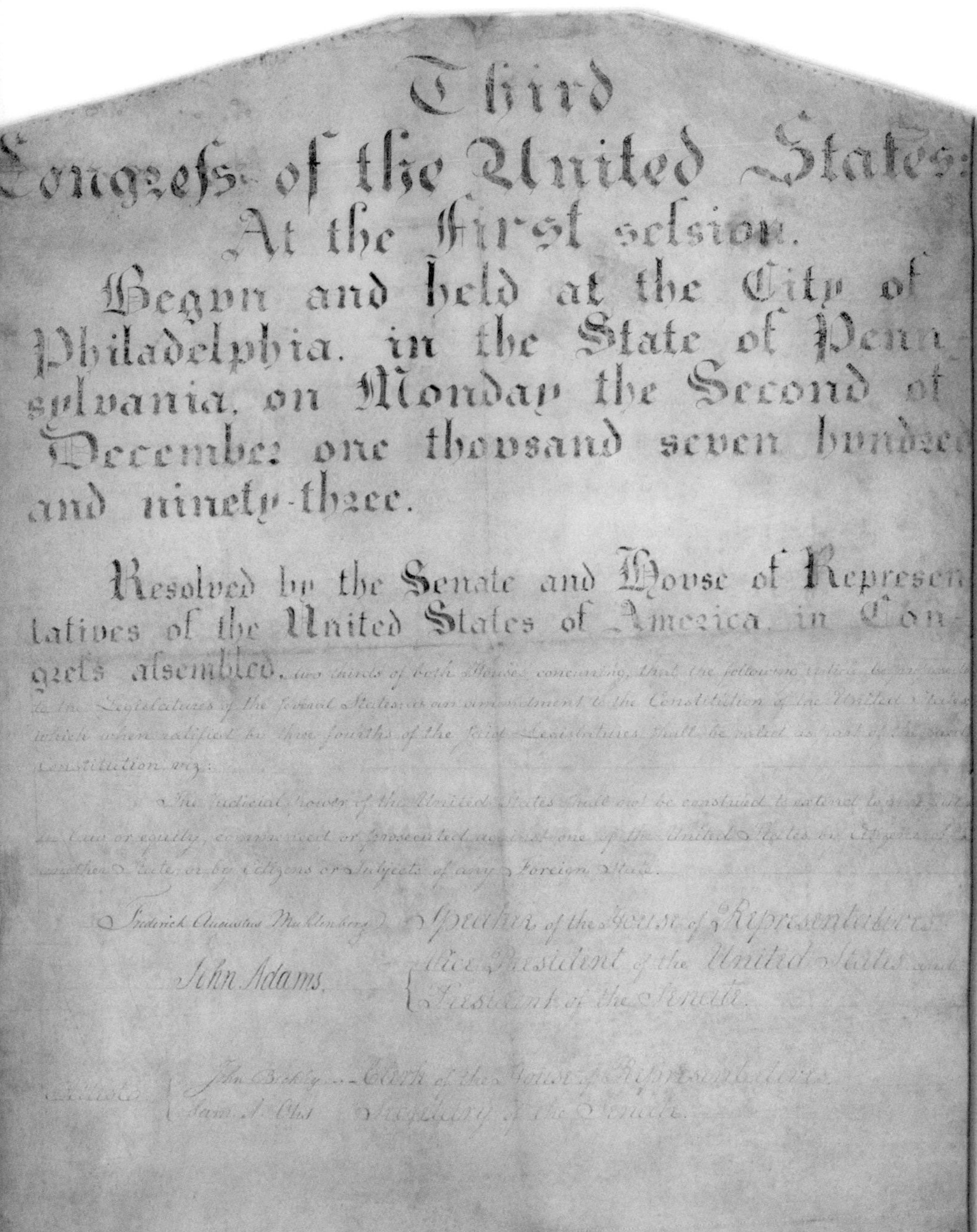

Third
Congress of the United States:
At the First session.
Begun and held at the City of Philadelphia, in the State of Pennsylvania, on Monday the Second of December one thousand seven hundred and ninety-three.

Resolved by the Senate and House of Representatives of the United States of America in Congress assembled, two thirds of both Houses concurring, that the following Article be proposed to the Legislatures of the several States, as an amendment to the Constitution of the United States, which when ratified by three fourths of the said Legislatures shall be valid as part of the said Constitution, viz:

The Judicial power of the United States shall not be construed to extend to any suit in law or equity, commenced or prosecuted against one of the United States by Citizens of another State, or by Citizens or Subjects of any Foreign State.

Frederick Augustus Muhlenberg, Speaker of the House of Representatives.
John Adams, Vice President of the United States and President of the Senate.

Attest, John Beckley, Clerk of the House of Representatives.
Sam. A. Otis Secretary of the Senate.

The Eleventh Amendment to the Constitution of the United States, ratified in 1795. NARA

in *Chisholm* v. *Georgia* (1793) permitted a suit brought by a citizen of South Carolina against the state of Georgia. Fearing that other states would follow suit, the amendment was proposed on March 4, 1794. It was ratified by 12 of the then 15 states on Feb. 7, 1795. South Carolina ratified the amendment in 1797; New Jersey and Pennsylvania did not ratify the amendment.

The full text of the Eleventh Amendment is:

> *The Judicial power of the United States shall not be construed to extend to any suit in law or equity, commenced or prosecuted against one of the United States by Citizens of another State, or by Citizens or Subjects of any Foreign State.*

TWELFTH AMENDMENT

The Twelfth Amendment (1804) to the Constitution of the United States revised presidential election procedures.

The catalyst for the Twelfth Amendment was the U.S. presidential election of 1800. Under the original text of the Constitution, political participation was at first reserved for the American elite. Only landowning white males could run for office and vote, and the voting privilege itself was restricted in presidential elections to elite slates of electors who would effectively choose the country's president and vice president. The framers had viewed political parties with suspicion, but by the 1790s party politics had taken root—and with it the interests of party organizations began to exert influence. In 1796 the Federalist Party supported John Adams for president, but it split its vote such that the Democratic-Republican candidate, Thomas Jefferson, earned the second greatest number of votes, thereby securing the post of vice president. To forestall this situation

EIGHTH *CONGRESS* OF THE UNITED STATES;

AT THE FIRST SESSION,

Begun and held at the city of Washington, in the territory of Columbia, on Monday, the seventeenth of October, one thousand eight hundred and three.

Resolved by the **Senate** and **House** of **Representatives** of the *United States* of *America*, in Congress assembled,

The Twelfth Amendment to the Constitution of the United States, ratified in 1804. NARA

from occurring again, the parties sought to ensure that all electors voted according to their party affiliation. In 1800 this produced an electoral college tie between Jefferson, the Democratic-Republican candidate for president, and Aaron Burr, the party's vice presidential candidate. Under the rules, the electors voted for two candidates without specifying who should hold which office. The election ultimately went to the House of Representatives, which elected Jefferson.

These elections revealed both a growing influence of political parties and a serious deficiency in the presidential election process. The effect of the Twelfth Amendment was to require separate votes for presidential and vice presidential candidates. Should an election result in a tie, the House of Representatives would chose for whom to cast votes, on the basis of a one-vote-per-state formulation, from among the top three electoral vote recipients. The Twelfth Amendment came into effect with the 1804 election.

The full text of the Twelfth Amendment is:

> *The electors shall meet in their respective states and vote by ballot for President and Vice President, one of whom, at least, shall not be an inhabitant of the same state with themselves; they shall name in their ballots the person voted for as President, and in distinct ballots the person voted for as Vice President, and they shall make distinct lists of all persons voted for as President, and of all persons voted for as Vice President, and of the number of votes for each, which lists they shall sign and certify, and transmit sealed to the seat of the government of the United States, directed to the President of the Senate;—The President of the Senate shall, in the presence of the Senate and House of Representatives, open all the certificates and the votes shall then be counted;—The person having the greatest number of votes for President, shall be the President,*

if such number be a majority of the whole number of Electors appointed; and if no person have such majority, then from the persons having the highest numbers not exceeding three on the list of those voted for as President, the House of Representatives shall choose immediately, by ballot, the President. But in choosing the President, the votes shall be taken by states, the representation from each state having one vote; a quorum for this purpose shall consist of a member or members from two-thirds of the states, and a majority of all the states shall be necessary to a choice. [And if the House of Representatives shall not choose a President whenever the right of choice shall devolve upon them, before the fourth day of March next following, then the Vice President shall act as President, as in the case of the death or other constitutional disability of the President.] The person having the greatest number of votes as Vice President, shall be the Vice President, if such number be a majority of the whole number of Electors appointed, and if no person have a majority, then from the two highest numbers on the list, the Senate shall choose the Vice President; a quorum for the purpose shall consist of two-thirds of the whole number of Senators, and a majority of the whole number shall be necessary to a choice. But no person constitutionally ineligible to the office of President shall be eligible to that of Vice President of the United States.*

* The part included in brackets has been superseded by Section 3 of the Twentieth Amendment.

THIRTEENTH AMENDMENT

The Thirteenth Amendment (1865) to the Constitution of the United States formally abolished slavery.

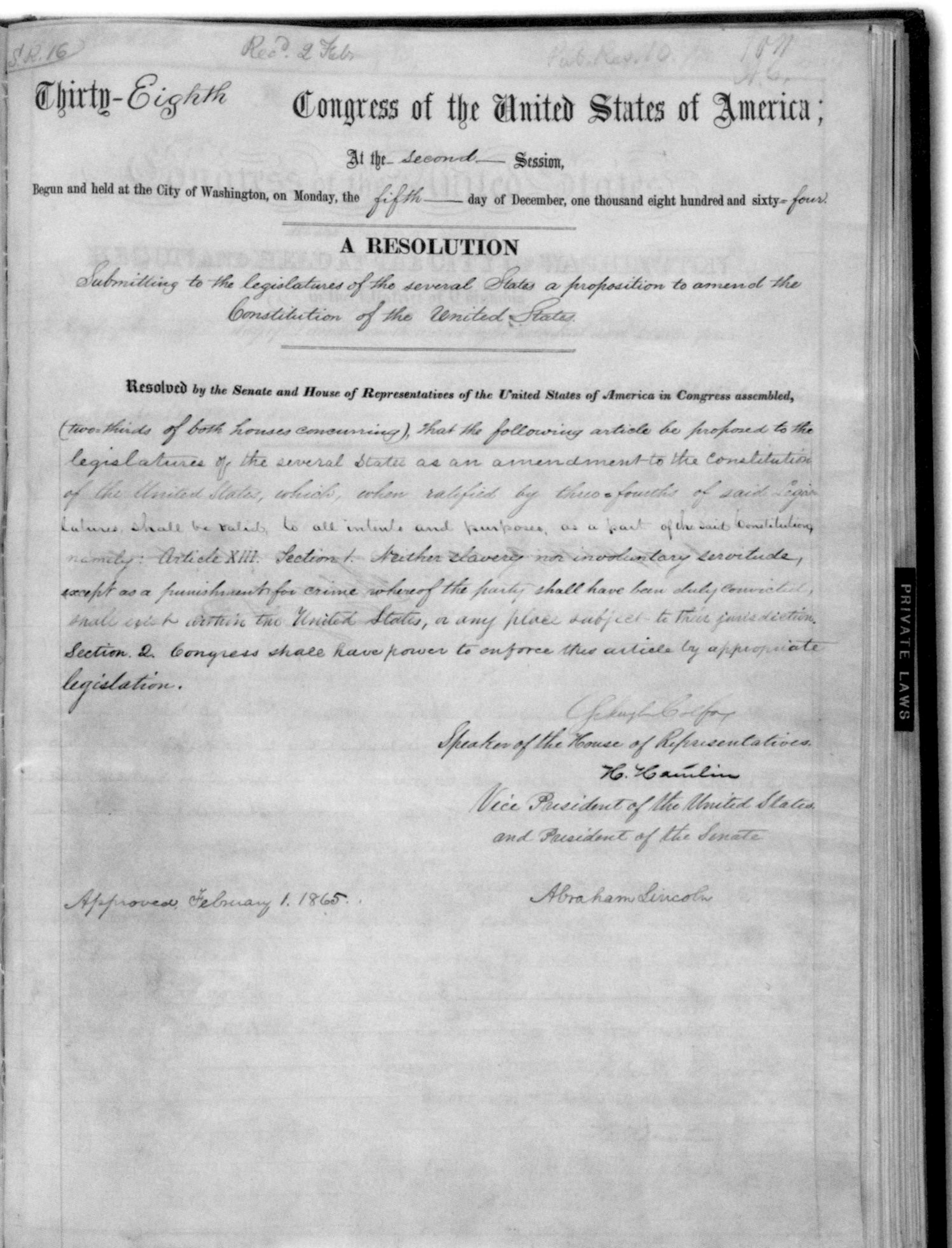

Thirty-Eighth Congress of the United States of America;

At the Second Session,

Begun and held at the City of Washington, on Monday, the fifth day of December, one thousand eight hundred and sixty-four.

A RESOLUTION

Submitting to the legislatures of the several States a proposition to amend the Constitution of the United States.

Resolved by the Senate and House of Representatives of the United States of America in Congress assembled, (two-thirds of both houses concurring), that the following article be proposed to the legislatures of the several States as an amendment to the Constitution of the United States, which, when ratified by three-fourths of said Legislatures, shall be valid, to all intents and purposes, as a part of the said Constitution, namely: Article XIII. Section 1. Neither slavery nor involuntary servitude, except as a punishment for crime whereof the party shall have been duly convicted, shall exist within the United States, or any place subject to their jurisdiction. Section 2. Congress shall have power to enforce this article by appropriate legislation.

Schuyler Colfax
Speaker of the House of Representatives.

H. Hamlin
Vice President of the United States and President of the Senate

Approved, February 1. 1865.

Abraham Lincoln

The Thirteenth Amendment to the Constitution of the United States, ratified in 1865. NARA

Although the words *slavery* and *slave* are never mentioned in the Constitution, the Thirteenth Amendment abrogated those sections of the Constitution that had tacitly codified the "peculiar institution": Article I, Section 2, regarding apportionment of representation in the House of Representatives, which had been "determined by adding to the whole Number of free Persons, including those bound to Service for a Term of Years, and excluding Indians not taxed, three fifths of all other Persons provided for the appointment," with "all other persons" meaning slaves; Article I, Section 9, which had established 1807 as the end date for the importation of slaves, referred to in this case as "such Persons as any of the States now existing shall think proper to admit"; and Article IV, Section 2, which mandated the return to their owners of fugitive slaves, here defined as persons

A celebration in the House of Representatives, Jan. 31, 1865, marking Congress's passing of the Thirteenth Amendment, which outlawed slavery. MPI/Archive Photos/Getty Images

"held to Service or Labour in one State, under the Laws thereof, escaping into another."

The Emancipation Proclamation, declared and promulgated by Pres. Abraham Lincoln in 1863 during the American Civil War, freed only those slaves held in the Confederate States of America. In depriving the South of its greatest economic resource—abundant free human labour—Lincoln's proclamation was intended primarily as an instrument of military strategy; only when emancipation was universally proposed through the Thirteenth Amendment did it become national policy. Moreover, the legality of abolition by presidential edict was questionable.

The amendment was passed by the Senate on April 8, 1864, but did not pass in the House until Jan. 31, 1865. The joint resolution of both bodies that submitted the amendment to the states for approval was signed by Lincoln on Feb. 1, 1865; however, he did not live to see its ratification. Shot by John Wilkes Booth, he died on April 15, 1865, and the amendment was not ratified by the required number of states until Dec. 6, 1865.

The full text of the Thirteenth Amendment is:

> *Neither slavery nor involuntary servitude, except as a punishment for crime whereof the party shall have been duly convicted, shall exist within the United States, or any place subject to their jurisdiction.*
>
> *Congress shall have power to enforce this article by appropriate legislation.*

FOURTEENTH AMENDMENT

The Fourteenth Amendment (1868) to the Constitution of the United States granted citizenship and equal civil and legal rights to African Americans and slaves who had been emancipated after the American Civil War, including them under the umbrella phrase "all persons born or naturalized in the United States." In all, the amendment comprises five sections, four of which began in 1866 as separate proposals that stalled in legislative process and were amalgamated into a single amendment.

This so-called Reconstruction Amendment prohibited the states from depriving any person of "life, liberty, or property, without due process of law" and from denying anyone within a state's jurisdiction equal protection under the law. Nullified by the Thirteenth Amendment, the section of the Constitution apportioning representation in the House of Representatives based on a formula that counted each slave as three-fifths of a person was replaced by a clause in the Fourteenth Amendment specifying that representatives be "apportioned among the several states according to their respective numbers, counting the whole number of persons in each state, excluding Indians not taxed." The amendment also prohibited former civil and military office holders who had supported the Confederacy from again holding any state or federal office—with the proviso that this prohibition could be removed from individuals by a two-thirds vote in both Houses of Congress. Moreover, the amendment upheld the national debt while exempting the federal government and state governments from any responsibility for the debts incurred by the rebellious Confederate States of America. Finally, the last section, mirroring the approach of the Thirteenth Amendment, provided for enforcement.

Among those legislators responsible for introducing the amendment's provisions were Rep. John A. Bingham of Ohio, Sen. Jacob Howard of Michigan, Rep. Henry Demig of Connecticut, Sen. Benjamin G. Brown of Missouri, and Rep. Thaddeus Stevens of Pennsylvania.

H.Res. 127. Rec'd 16. June.

Thirty-ninth Congress of the United States, at the first session, begun and held at the City of Washington, in the District of Columbia, on Monday the fourth day of December, one thousand eight hundred and sixty-five.

Joint Resolution proposing an amendment to the Constitution of the United States.

Be it resolved by the Senate and House of Representatives of the United States of America in Congress assembled, (two thirds of both Houses concurring,) That the following article be proposed to the legislatures of the several States as an amendment to the Constitution of the United States, which, when ratified by three fourths of said legislatures, shall be valid as part of the Constitution, namely:

Article XIV.

Section 1. All persons born or naturalized in the United States, and subject to the jurisdiction thereof, are citizens of the United States and of the State wherein they reside. No State shall make or enforce any law which shall abridge the privileges or immunities of citizens of the United States; nor shall any State deprive any person of life, liberty, or property, without due process of law; nor deny to any person within its jurisdiction the equal protection of the laws.

Section 2. Representatives shall be apportioned among the several States according to their respective numbers, counting the whole number of persons in each State, excluding Indians not taxed. But when the right to vote at any election for the choice of electors for President and Vice President of the United States, Representatives in Congress, the Executive and Judicial officers of a State, or the members of the Legislature thereof, is denied to any of the male inhabitants of such State, being twenty-one years of age, and citizens of the United States, or in any way abridged, except for participation in rebellion, or other crime, the basis of representation therein shall be reduced in the proportion which the

The first page of the Fourteenth Amendment to the Constitution of the United States, ratified in 1868. NARA

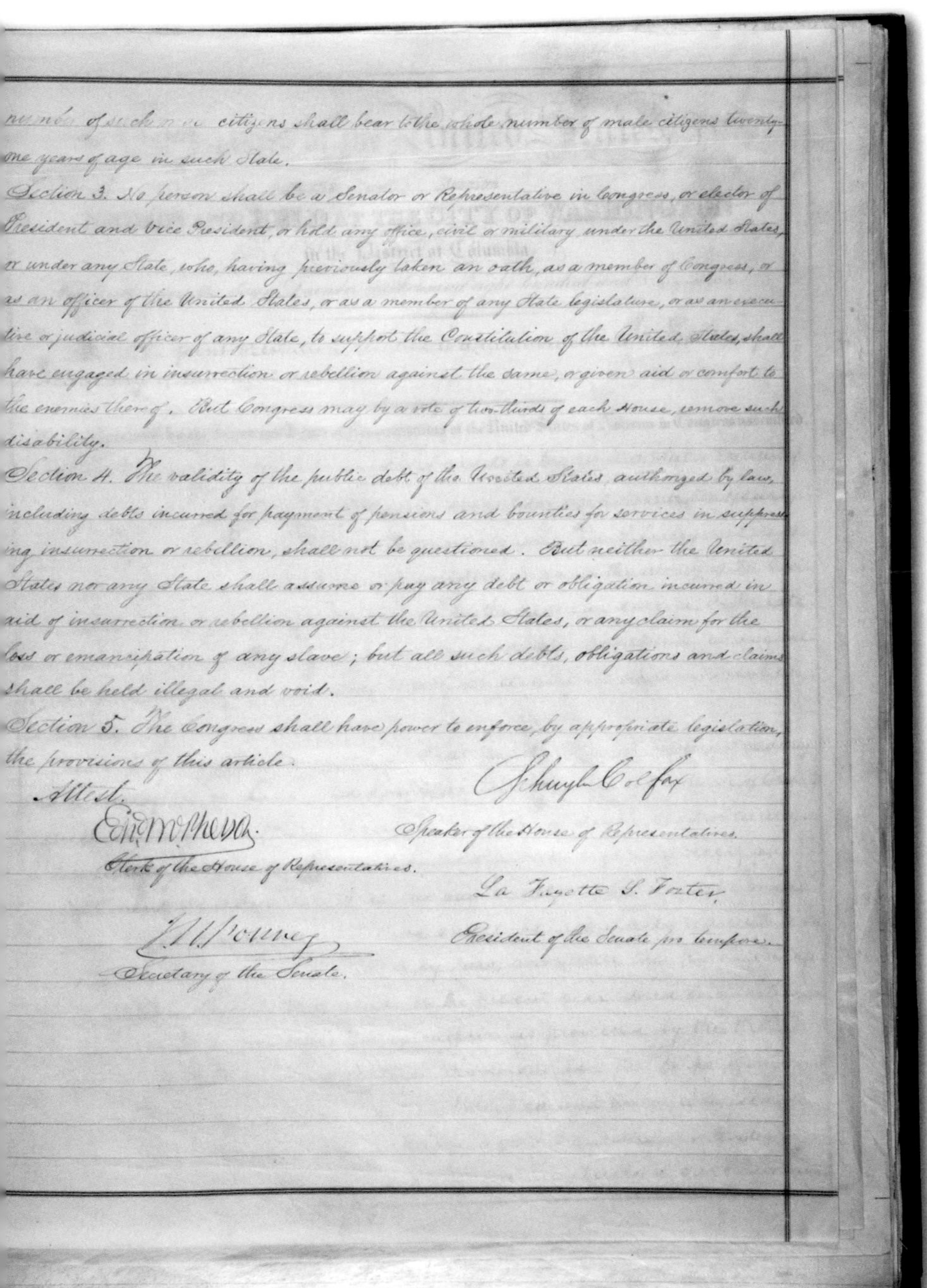

number of such male citizens shall bear to the whole number of male citizens twenty-one years of age in such State.

Section 3. No person shall be a Senator or Representative in Congress, or elector of President and Vice President, or hold any office, civil or military, under the United States, or under any State, who, having previously taken an oath, as a member of Congress, or as an officer of the United States, or as a member of any State legislature, or as an executive or judicial officer of any State, to support the Constitution of the United States, shall have engaged in insurrection or rebellion against the same, or given aid or comfort to the enemies thereof. But Congress may by a vote of two-thirds of each House, remove such disability.

Section 4. The validity of the public debt of the United States, authorized by law, including debts incurred for payment of pensions and bounties for services in suppressing insurrection or rebellion, shall not be questioned. But neither the United States nor any State shall assume or pay any debt or obligation incurred in aid of insurrection or rebellion against the United States, or any claim for the loss or emancipation of any slave; but all such debts, obligations and claims shall be held illegal and void.

Section 5. The Congress shall have power to enforce, by appropriate legislation, the provisions of this article.

Schuyler Colfax

Speaker of the House of Representatives.

Attest.

Edw. McPherson

Clerk of the House of Representatives.

La Fayette S. Foster

President of the Senate pro tempore.

J. W. Forney

Secretary of the Senate.

The second page of the Fourteenth Amendment to the Constitution of the United States, ratified in 1868. NARA

The Congressional Joint Resolution proposing the amendment was submitted to the states for ratification on June 16, 1866. On July 28, 1868, having been ratified by the requisite number of states, it entered into force. However, its attempt to guarantee civil rights was circumvented for many decades by the post-Reconstruction-era black codes, Jim Crow laws, and the "separate but equal" ruling of *Plessy* v. *Ferguson* (1896).

The full text of the Fourteenth Amendment is:

> *All persons born or naturalized in the United States, and subject to the jurisdiction thereof, are citizens of the United States and of the state wherein they reside. No state shall make or enforce any law which shall abridge the privileges or immunities of citizens of the United States; nor shall any state deprive any person of life, liberty, or property, without due process of law; nor deny to any person within its jurisdiction the equal protection of the laws.*

> *Representatives shall be apportioned among the several states according to their respective numbers, counting the whole number of persons in each state, excluding Indians not taxed. But when the right to vote at any election for the choice of electors for President and Vice President of the United States, Representatives in Congress, the executive and judicial officers of a state, or the members of the legislature thereof, is denied to any of the male inhabitants of such state, being twenty-one years of age, and citizens of the United States, or in any way abridged, except for participation in rebellion, or other crime,*

the basis of representation therein shall be reduced in the proportion which the number of such male citizens shall bear to the whole number of male citizens twenty-one years of age in such state.

No person shall be a Senator or Representative in Congress, or elector of President and Vice President, or hold any office, civil or military, under the United States, or under any state, who, having previously taken an oath, as a member of Congress, or as an officer of the United States, or as a member of any state legislature, or as an executive or judicial officer of any state, to support the Constitution of the United States, shall have engaged in insurrection or rebellion against the same, or given aid or comfort to the enemies thereof. But Congress may by a vote of two-thirds of each House, remove such disability.

The validity of the public debt of the United States, authorized by law, including debts incurred for payment of pensions and bounties for services in suppressing insurrection or rebellion, shall not be questioned. But neither the United States nor any state shall assume or pay any debt or obligation incurred in aid of insurrection or rebellion against the United States, or any claim for the loss or emancipation of any slave; but all such debts, obligations and claims shall be held illegal and void.

The Congress shall have power to enforce, by appropriate legislation, the provisions of this article.

RECONSTRUCTION

Reconstruction is the name given to the period (1865–77) after the American Civil War in which attempts were made to solve the political, social, and economic problems arising from the readmission to the Union of the 11 Confederate states that had seceded at or before the outbreak of war. Pres. Abraham Lincoln planned to readmit states in which at least 10 percent of the voters had pledged loyalty to the Union. This lenient approach was opposed by the Radical Republicans, who favoured the harsher measures passed in the Wade-Davis Bill. Pres. Andrew Johnson continued Lincoln's moderate policies, but enactment in the South of the black codes and demand in the North for stricter legislation resulted in victories for Radical Republicans in the congressional elections of 1866. Congress then passed the Reconstruction Acts of 1867, which established military districts in the South and required the Southern states to accept the Fourteenth and Fifteenth Amendments to the Constitution. Southern resentment of the imposed state governments, which included Republicans, carpetbaggers, and scalawags, and of the activities of the Freedmen's Bureau, led to the formation of terrorist groups such as the Ku Klux Klan and the Knights of the White Camelia. By the 1870s conservative Democrats again controlled most state governments in the South. Although Reconstruction has been seen as a period of corruption, many constructive legal and educational reforms were introduced. The Reconstruction era led to an increase in sectional bitterness, dissension regarding the rights of African- Americans, and the development of one-party politics in the South.

S.R. 8.

Pub. Res. 10

Fortieth Congress of the United States of America;

At the third Session,

Begun and held at the city of Washington, on Monday, the seventh day of December, one thousand eight hundred and sixty-eight.

A RESOLUTION

Proposing an amendment to the Constitution of the United States.

Resolved by the Senate and House of Representatives of the United States of America in Congress assembled, (two-thirds of both Houses concurring) That the following article be proposed to the legislatures of the several States as an amendment to the Constitution of the United States, which when ratified by three-fourths of said legislatures shall be valid as part of the Constitution, namely:

Article XV.

Section 1. The right of citizens of the United States to vote shall not be denied or abridged by the United States or by any State on account of race, color, or previous condition of servitude—

Section 2. The Congress shall have power to enforce this article by appropriate legislation—

Schuyler Colfax

Speaker of the House of Representatives.

B. F. Wade

President of the Senate pro tempore.

Attest:

Edw. McPherson

Clerk of House of Representatives.

Geo. C. Gorham

Secy of Senate U.S.

The Fifteenth Amendment to the Constitution of the United States, ratified in 1870. NARA

FIFTEENTH AMENDMENT

The Fifteenth Amendment (1870) to the Constitution of the United States guaranteed that the right to vote could not be denied based on "race, color, or previous condition of servitude."

The amendment complemented and followed in the wake of the passage of the Thirteenth and Fourteenth amendments, which abolished slavery and guaranteed citizenship, respectively, to African-Americans. The passage of the amendment and its subsequent ratification (Feb. 3, 1870) effectively enfranchised African-American men, while denying the right to vote to women of all colors.

The Fifteenth Amendment, Celebrated May 19th 1870, *lithograph with watercolour by Thomas Kelly, c. 1870.* Library of Congress, Washington, D.C. (Digital File Number: cph 3g02399)

Women would not receive that right until the ratification of the Nineteenth Amendment in 1920.

After the Civil War, during Reconstruction (1865–77), the amendment was successful in encouraging African-Americans to vote. Many African-Americans were even elected to public office during the 1880s in the states that formerly had constituted the Confederate States of America. By the 1890s, however, efforts by several states to enact such measures as poll taxes, literacy tests, and grandfather clauses—in addition to widespread threats and violence—had completely reversed these trends. By the beginning of the 20th century, nearly all African-Americans in the states of the former Confederacy were again disenfranchised. Although the Supreme Court and Congress attempted to strike down such actions as unconstitutional, it was not until Pres. Lyndon B. Johnson introduced the Voting Rights Act of 1965 that Congress was able to put an end to this violence and discrimination. The act abolished voter prerequisites and allowed for federal supervision of voter registration. With the passage of the Voting Rights Act, the Fifteenth Amendment was finally enforceable, and voter turnout among African-Americans improved markedly.

The full text of the Fifteenth Amendment is:

> *The right of citizens of the United States to vote shall not be denied or abridged by the United States or by any State on account of race, color, or previous condition of servitude—*

> *The Congress shall have power to enforce this article by appropriate legislation.*

SIXTEENTH AMENDMENT

The Sixteenth Amendment (1913) to the Constitution of the United States permitted a federal income tax. Article I, Section 8, of the Constitution empowers Congress to "lay and collect Taxes, Duties, Imposts and Excises, to pay the Debts and provide for the common Defence and general Welfare of the United States; but all Duties, Imposts and Excises shall be uniform throughout the United States." Article I, Section 9, further states that "No Capitation, or other direct, Tax shall be laid, unless in Proportion to the Census or Enumeration herein before directed to be taken." Although income taxes levied in support of the American Civil War (1861–65) were generally tolerated, subsequent attempts by Congress to impose taxes on income were met with significant opposition. In 1895, in *Pollock* v. *Farmers' Loan and Trust Company*, the U.S. Supreme Court declared the federal income tax unconstitutional in striking down portions of the Wilson-Gorman Tariff Act of 1894 that imposed a direct tax on the incomes of American citizens and corporations. It thereby made any direct tax subject to the rules articulated in Article I, Section 2. Consequently, unless the U.S. Congress expected all income taxes to be apportioned among the states according to their populations, the power to levy income taxes was rendered impotent. The Sixteenth Amendment was introduced in 1909 to remedy this problem. By specifically affixing the language, "from whatever source derived," it removes the "direct tax dilemma" related to Article I, Section 8, and authorizes Congress to lay and collect income tax without regard to the rules of Article I, Section 9, regarding census and enumeration.

The full text of the Sixteenth Amendment is:

The Congress shall have power to lay and collect taxes on incomes, from whatever source derived,

S. J. Res. 40.

Sixty-first Congress of the United States of America;

At the First Session,

Begun and held at the City of Washington on Monday, the fifteenth day of March, one thousand nine hundred and nine.

JOINT RESOLUTION

Proposing an amendment to the Constitution of the United States.

Resolved by the Senate and House of Representatives of the United States of America in Congress assembled (two-thirds of each House concurring therein), That the following article is proposed as an amendment to the Constitution of the United States, which, when ratified by the legislatures of three-fourths of the several States, shall be valid to all intents and purposes as a part of the Constitution:

"Article XVI. The Congress shall have power to lay and collect taxes on incomes, from whatever source derived, without apportionment among the several States, and without regard to any census or enumeration."

Speaker of the House of Representatives.

Vice-President of the United States and President of the Senate.

The Sixteenth Amendment to the Constitution of the United States, ratified in 1913. NARA

without apportionment among the several States, and without regard to any census or enumeration.

SEVENTEENTH AMENDMENT

The Seventeenth Amendment (1913) to the Constitution of the United States provided for the direct election of U.S. senators by the voters of the states. The Seventeenth Amendment altered the electoral mechanism established in Article I, Section 3 of the Constitution, which had provided for the appointment of senators by the state legislatures. Adopted in the Progressive era of democratic political reform, the amendment reflected popular dissatisfaction with the corruption and inefficiency that had come to characterize the legislative election of U.S. senators in many states.

The amendment changed the wording of Article I, Section 3, Paragraph 1 to state that "two Senators from each State" should be "elected by the people thereof" rather than "chosen by the Legislature thereof." It also revised Paragraph 2 of Section 3 to allow the state executive to fill vacancies in the Senate by making temporary appointments to serve until new elections could be held.

By the time of the amendment's adoption, many states had already established mechanisms that effectively allowed voters to choose the senators of their state (e.g., by having the legislature appoint the winners of party primaries). Nevertheless, the amendment was widely seen as necessary to reduce the influence of big business and other special interests on the selection of senators and to prevent vacancies or frequent turnover in the Senate caused by party wrangling or changes of party leadership at the state level. Beginning in the late 20th century some conservative political scholars called for the repeal of the Seventeenth Amendment on the grounds that it undermined the proper balance of power

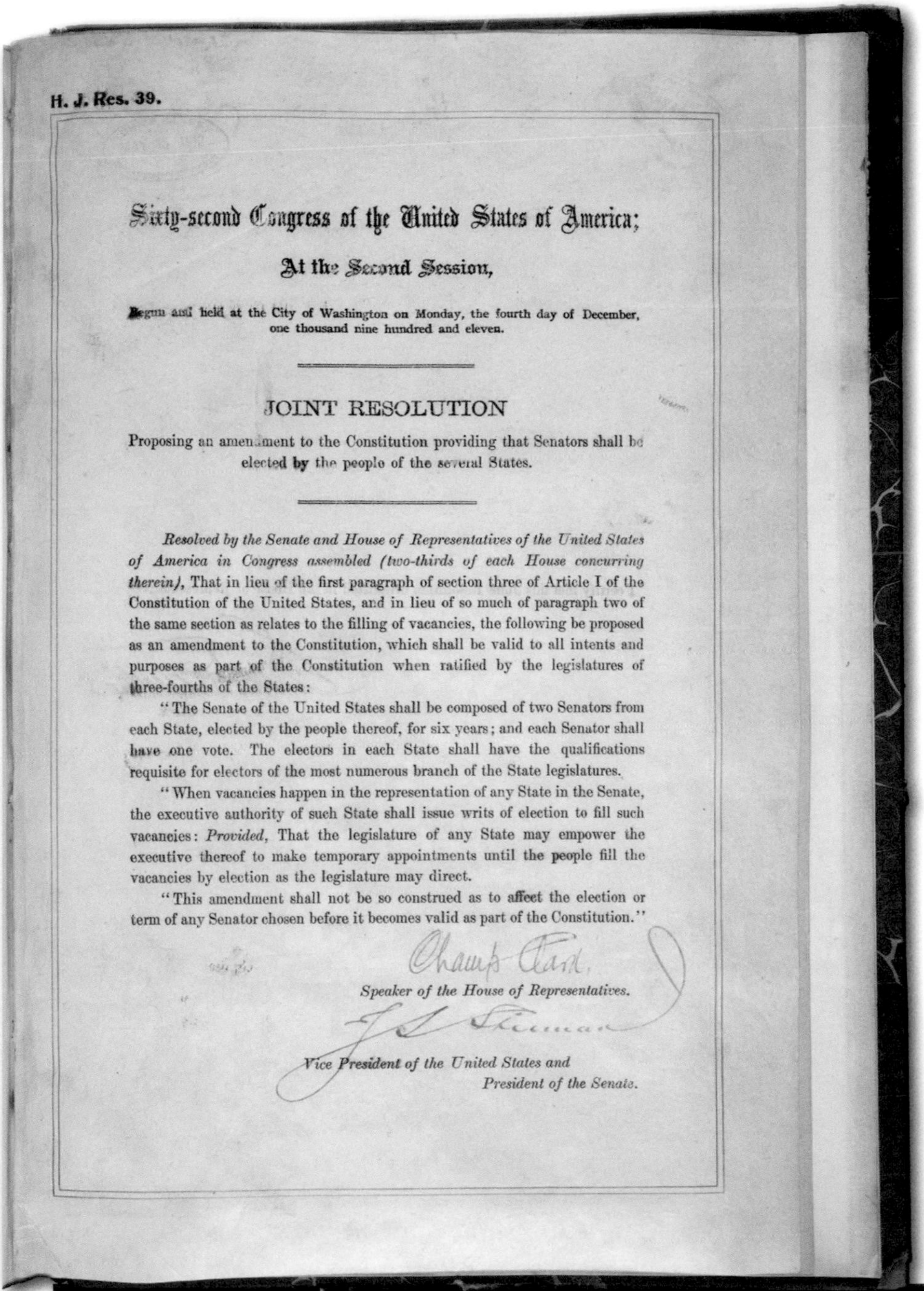

H. J. Res. 39.

Sixty-second Congress of the United States of America;

At the Second Session,

Begun and held at the City of Washington on Monday, the fourth day of December, one thousand nine hundred and eleven.

JOINT RESOLUTION

Proposing an amendment to the Constitution providing that Senators shall be elected by the people of the several States.

Resolved by the Senate and House of Representatives of the United States of America in Congress assembled (two-thirds of each House concurring therein), That in lieu of the first paragraph of section three of Article I of the Constitution of the United States, and in lieu of so much of paragraph two of the same section as relates to the filling of vacancies, the following be proposed as an amendment to the Constitution, which shall be valid to all intents and purposes as part of the Constitution when ratified by the legislatures of three-fourths of the States:

"The Senate of the United States shall be composed of two Senators from each State, elected by the people thereof, for six years; and each Senator shall have one vote. The electors in each State shall have the qualifications requisite for electors of the most numerous branch of the State legislatures.

"When vacancies happen in the representation of any State in the Senate, the executive authority of such State shall issue writs of election to fill such vacancies: *Provided,* That the legislature of any State may empower the executive thereof to make temporary appointments until the people fill the vacancies by election as the legislature may direct.

"This amendment shall not be so construed as to affect the election or term of any Senator chosen before it becomes valid as part of the Constitution."

Champ Clark.

Speaker of the House of Representatives.

J S Sherman

Vice President of the United States and President of the Senate.

The Seventeenth Amendment to the Constitution of the United States, ratified in 1913. NARA

between the federal government and the states.

The full text of the Seventeenth Amendment is:

> *The Senate of the United States shall be composed of two Senators from each State, elected by the people thereof, for six years; and each Senator shall have one vote. The electors in each State shall have the qualifications requisite for electors of the most numerous branch of the State legislatures.*

> *When vacancies happen in the representation of any State in the Senate, the executive authority of such State shall issue writs of election to fill such vacancies: Provided, That the legislature of any State may empower the executive thereof to make temporary appointments until the people fill the vacancies by election as the legislature may direct.*

> *This amendment shall not be so construed as to affect the election or term of any Senator chosen before it becomes valid as part of the Constitution.*

EIGHTEENTH AMENDMENT

The Eighteenth Amendment (1919) to the Constitution of the United States imposed a federal prohibition of alcohol.

The Eighteenth Amendment emerged from the organized efforts of the temperance movement and the Anti-Saloon League, which attributed to alcohol virtually all of society's ills and led campaigns at the local, state, and national levels to combat its manufacture, sale, distribution, and consumption. Most of the organized

S. J. Res. 17.

Sixty-fifth Congress of the United States of America;

At the Second Session,

Begun and held at the City of Washington on Monday, the third day of December, one thousand nine hundred and seventeen.

JOINT RESOLUTION

Proposing an amendment to the Constitution of the United States.

Resolved by the Senate and House of Representatives of the United States of America in Congress assembled (two-thirds of each House concurring therein), That the following amendment to the Constitution be, and hereby is, proposed to the States, to become valid as a part of the Constitution when ratified by the legislatures of the several States as provided by the Constitution:

"ARTICLE —.

"SECTION 1. After one year from the ratification of this article the manufacture, sale, or transportation of intoxicating liquors within, the importation thereof into, or the exportation thereof from the United States and all territory subject to the jurisdiction thereof for beverage purposes is hereby prohibited.

"SEC. 2. The Congress and the several States shall have concurrent power to enforce this article by appropriate legislation.

"SEC. 3. This article shall be inoperative unless it shall have been ratified as an amendment to the Constitution by the legislatures of the several States, as provided in the Constitution, within seven years from the date of the submission hereof to the States by the Congress."

Champ Clark

Speaker of the House of Representatives.

Thos. R. Marshall

Vice President of the United States and President of the Senate.

The Eighteenth Amendment to the Constitution of the United States, ratified in 1919. NARA

efforts supporting Prohibition involved religious coalitions that linked alcohol to immorality, criminality, and, with the advent of World War I, unpatriotic citizenship. The amendment passed both chambers of the U.S. Congress in December 1917 and was ratified by the requisite three-fourths of the states in January 1919. Its language called for Congress to pass enforcement legislation, and this was championed by Andrew Volstead, chairman of the House Judiciary Committee, who engineered passage of the National Prohibition Act (commonly referred to as the Volstead Act). The act was conceived by Anti-Saloon League leader Wayne Wheeler and passed over the veto of Pres. Woodrow Wilson.

Neither the Volstead Act nor the amendment was enforced with great success. Indeed, entire illegal economies (bootlegging, speakeasies, and distilling operations) flourished. The public appetite for alcohol remained and was only intensified with the stock market crash of 1929. In March 1933, shortly after taking office, Pres. Franklin D. Roosevelt signed the Cullen-Harrison Act, which amended the Volstead Act, permitting the manufacturing and sale of low-alcohol beer and wines (up to 3.2 percent alcohol by volume). Nine months later, on Dec. 5, 1933, federal prohibition was repealed with the ratification of the Twenty-first Amendment (which allowed Prohibition to be maintained at the state and local levels). The Eighteenth Amendment is the only amendment to have been repealed.

The full text of the Eighteenth Amendment is:

> *Section 1—After one year from the ratification of this article the manufacture, sale, or transportation of intoxicating liquors within, the importation thereof into, or the exportation thereof from the United States and all territory subject to the jurisdiction thereof for beverage purposes is hereby prohibited.*

Section 2—The Congress and the several States shall have concurrent power to enforce this article by appropriate legislation.

Section 3—This article shall be inoperative unless it shall have been ratified as an amendment to the Constitution by the legislatures of the several States, as provided in the Constitution, within seven years from the date of the submission hereof to the States by the Congress.

NINETEENTH AMENDMENT

The Nineteenth Amendment (1920) to the Constitution of the United States officially extended the right to vote to women.

Opposition to woman suffrage in the United States predated the Constitutional Convention (1787), which drafted and adopted the Constitution. The prevailing view within society was that women should be precluded from holding office and voting—indeed, it was generally accepted (among men) that women should be protected from the evils of politics. Still, there was opposition to such patriarchal views from the beginning, as when Abigail Adams, wife of John Adams, asked her husband in 1776, as he went to the Continental Congress to adopt the Declaration of Independence, to "remember the ladies and be more generous and favorable to them than your ancestors." In the scattered places where women could vote in some types of local elections, they began to lose this right in the late 18th century.

From the founding of the United States, women were almost universally excluded from voting and their voices

H. J. Res. 1.

Sixty-sixth Congress of the United States of America;

At the First Session,

Begun and held at the City of Washington on Monday, the nineteenth day of May, one thousand nine hundred and nineteen.

JOINT RESOLUTION

Proposing an amendment to the Constitution extending the right of suffrage to women.

Resolved by the Senate and House of Representatives of the United States of America in Congress assembled (two-thirds of each House concurring therein), That the following article is proposed as an amendment to the Constitution, which shall be valid to all intents and purposes as part of the Constitution when ratified by the legislatures of three-fourths of the several States.

"ARTICLE ———.

"The right of citizens of the United States to vote shall not be denied or abridged by the United States or by any State on account of sex.

"Congress shall have power to enforce this article by appropriate legislation."

F. H. Gillett

Speaker of the House of Representatives.

Thos. R. Marshall

Vice President of the United States and President of the Senate.

The Nineteenth Amendment to the Constitution of the United States, ratified in 1920. NARA

largely suppressed from the political sphere. Beginning in the early 19th century, as women chafed at these restrictions, the movement for woman suffrage began and was tied in large part to agitation against slavery. In July 1848 in Seneca Falls, N.Y., then the hometown of Elizabeth Cady Stanton, the Seneca Falls Convention launched the women's rights movement and called for woman suffrage. The American Civil War (1861–65) resulted in the end of the institution of slavery, and in its aftermath many women abolitionists put on hold their desire for universal suffrage in favour of ensuring suffrage for newly freed male slaves.

Gradually throughout the second half of the 19th century, certain states and territories extended often limited voting rights to women. Wyoming Territory granted women the right to vote in all elections in 1869. But it soon became apparent that an amendment to the federal Constitution would be a preferable plan for suffragists. Two organizations were formed in 1869: the National Woman Suffrage Association, which sought to achieve a federal constitutional amendment that would secure the ballot for women; and the American Woman Suffrage Association, which focused on obtaining amendments to that effect in the constitutions of the various states. The two organizations worked together closely and would merge in 1890.

In 1878 a constitutional amendment was introduced in Congress that would enshrine woman suffrage for all elections. It would be reintroduced in every Congress thereafter. In 1890 Wyoming became a state and thus also became the first state whose constitution guaranteed women the right to vote. Over the next decade several other states—all in the western part of the country—joined Wyoming. In 1912, when Theodore Roosevelt ran (unsuccessfully) as a third-party candidate for president (he had already served in that office from 1901 to 1909), his party became the first national party to adopt a plank supporting a constitutional amendment.

In January 1918, with momentum clearly behind the suffragists—15 states had extended equal voting rights to women, and the amendment was formally supported by both parties and by the president, Woodrow Wilson—the amendment passed with the bare minimum two-thirds support in the House of Representatives, but it failed narrowly in the U.S. Senate. This galvanized the National Woman's Party, which led a campaign seeking to oust senators who had voted against it.

A subsequent attempt to pass the amendment came in 1919, and this time it passed both chambers with the requisite two-thirds majority—304–89 in the House of Representatives on May 21, and 56–25 in the Senate on

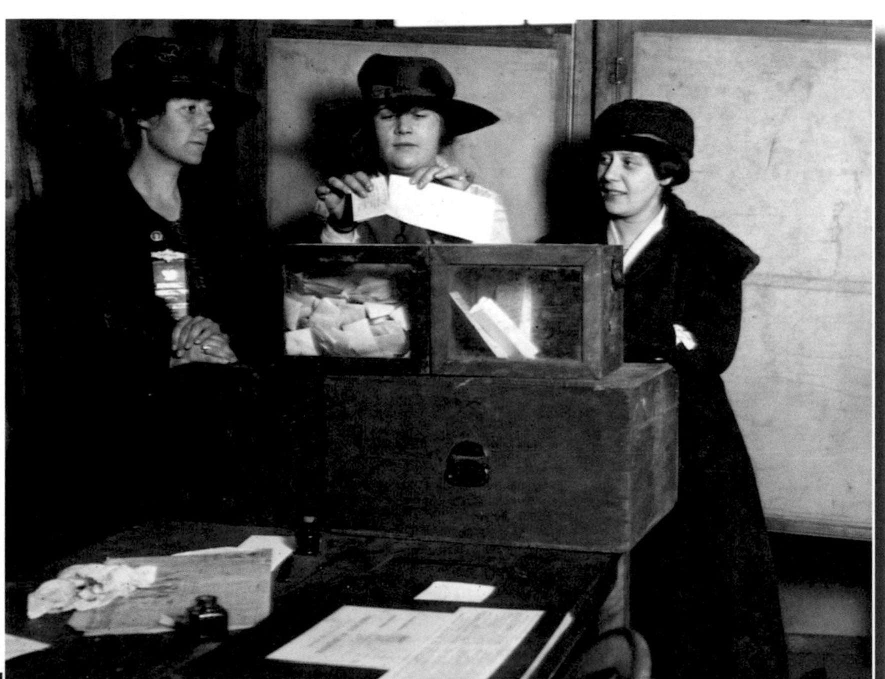

Women casting their votes in New York City, c. 1920s. Library of Congress, Washington, D.C. (digital file no. 00037)

June 4. Although the amendment's fate seemed in doubt because of opposition throughout much of the South, on Aug. 18, 1920, Tennessee—by one vote—became the 36th state to ratify the amendment, thereby ensuring its adoption. On August 26 the Nineteenth Amendment was proclaimed by the secretary of state as being part of the Constitution of the United States.

The full text of the Nineteenth Amendment is:

> *The right of citizens of the United States to vote shall not be denied or abridged by the United States or by any State on account of sex.*
>
> *Congress shall have power to enforce this article by appropriate legislation.*

TWENTIETH AMENDMENT

The Twentieth Amendment (1933) to the Constitution of the United States fixed the beginning and ending dates of presidential and congressional terms. The amendment was proposed by Sen. George W. Norris of Nebraska on March 2, 1932, and was certified the following January.

Commonly known as the "Lame Duck Amendment," the Twentieth Amendment was designed to remove the excessively long period of time a defeated president or member of Congress would continue to serve after his or her failed bid for reelection. Originally, federal officials took their seats on March 4 (the date coinciding with the government's commencement of proceedings in 1789), four months after election day, and per Article I, section 4, members of Congress "shall assemble at least once in every Year, and such Meeting

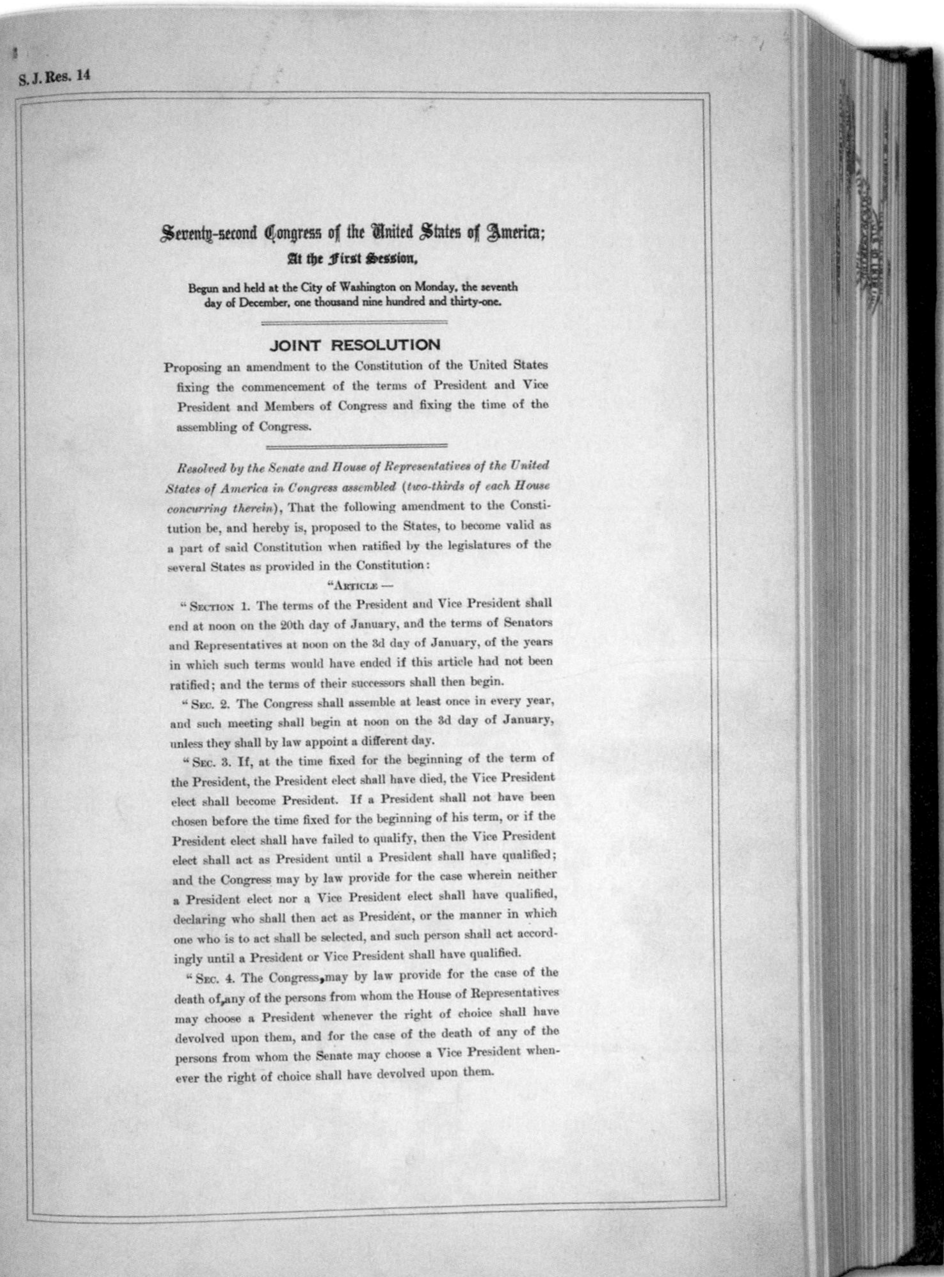

S. J. Res. 14

Seventy-second Congress of the United States of America;
At the First Session,

Begun and held at the City of Washington on Monday, the seventh day of December, one thousand nine hundred and thirty-one.

JOINT RESOLUTION

Proposing an amendment to the Constitution of the United States fixing the commencement of the terms of President and Vice President and Members of Congress and fixing the time of the assembling of Congress.

Resolved by the Senate and House of Representatives of the United States of America in Congress assembled (two-thirds of each House concurring therein), That the following amendment to the Constitution be, and hereby is, proposed to the States, to become valid as a part of said Constitution when ratified by the legislatures of the several States as provided in the Constitution:

"Article —

"Section 1. The terms of the President and Vice President shall end at noon on the 20th day of January, and the terms of Senators and Representatives at noon on the 3d day of January, of the years in which such terms would have ended if this article had not been ratified; and the terms of their successors shall then begin.

"Sec. 2. The Congress shall assemble at least once in every year, and such meeting shall begin at noon on the 3d day of January, unless they shall by law appoint a different day.

"Sec. 3. If, at the time fixed for the beginning of the term of the President, the President elect shall have died, the Vice President elect shall become President. If a President shall not have been chosen before the time fixed for the beginning of his term, or if the President elect shall have failed to qualify, then the Vice President elect shall act as President until a President shall have qualified; and the Congress may by law provide for the case wherein neither a President elect nor a Vice President elect shall have qualified, declaring who shall then act as President, or the manner in which one who is to act shall be selected, and such person shall act accordingly until a President or Vice President shall have qualified.

"Sec. 4. The Congress, may by law provide for the case of the death of, any of the persons from whom the House of Representatives may choose a President whenever the right of choice shall have devolved upon them, and for the case of the death of any of the persons from whom the Senate may choose a Vice President whenever the right of choice shall have devolved upon them.

The first page of the Twentieth Amendment to the Constitution of the United States, ratified in 1933. NARA

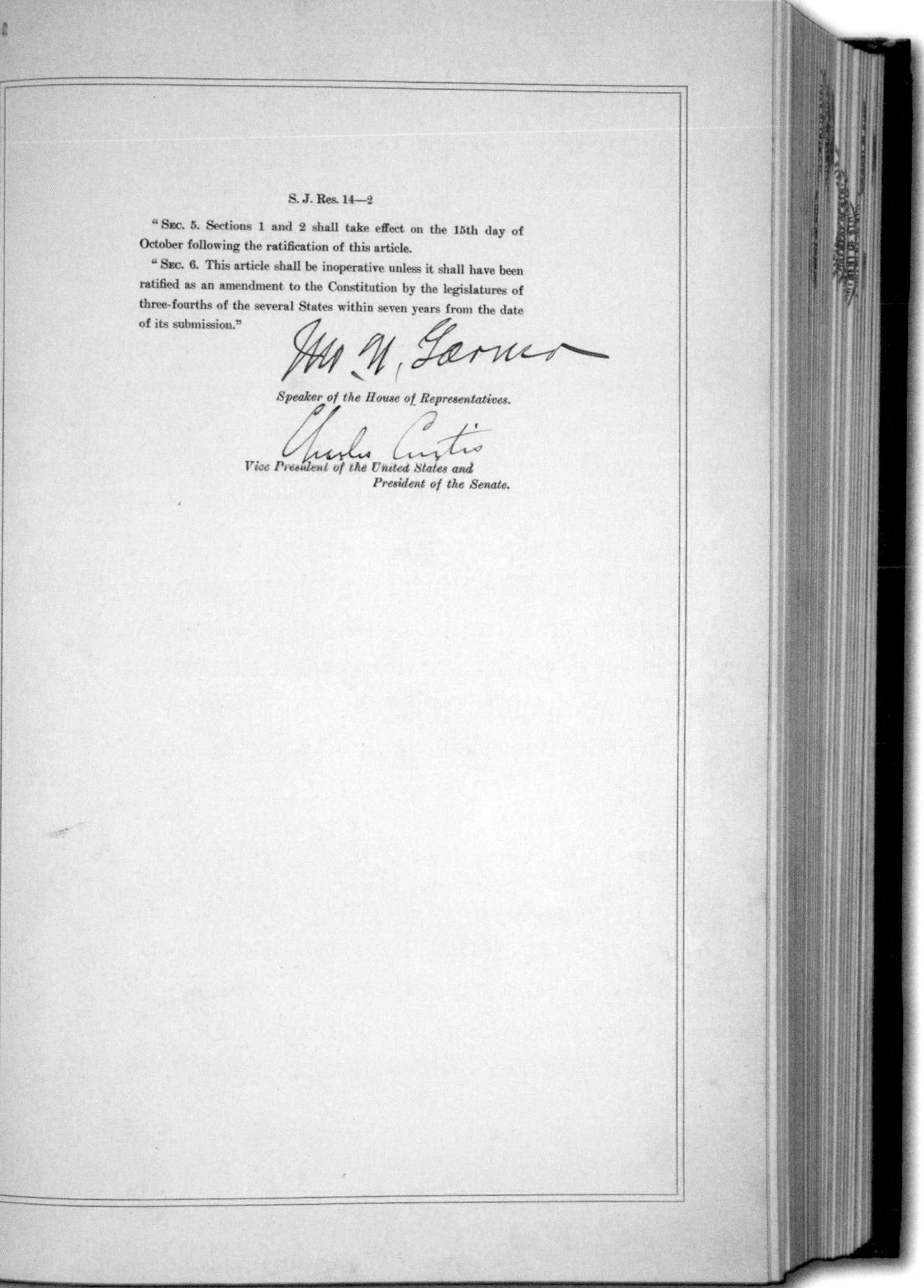

S. J. Res. 14—2

"Sec. 5. Sections 1 and 2 shall take effect on the 15th day of October following the ratification of this article.

"Sec. 6. This article shall be inoperative unless it shall have been ratified as an amendment to the Constitution by the legislatures of three-fourths of the several States within seven years from the date of its submission."

Jno. N. Garner

Speaker of the House of Representatives.

Charles Curtis

Vice President of the United States and President of the Senate.

The second page of the Twentieth Amendment to the Constitution of the United States, ratified in 1933. NARA

shall be on the first Monday in December, unless they shall by Law appoint a different Day"; this meant that it would be 13 months before a new Congress met, and there would be a necessary session of Congress following the November elections. Because they were voted out of office, defeated politicians would serve as lame ducks, incapable of effectively representing their constituents or affecting public policy. Critics, particularly those in the Progressive movement that had been vital to other political reforms, argued that shrinking the gap in time between elections and taking office amounted to an immediate call to public service. The amendment also provided for the vice president-elect to become president if a president-elect died before taking the oath of office. The third and fourth sections of the Amendment (pertaining to death, disability, disqualification, and succession) are addressed further in the Twenty-fifth Amendment.

The full text of the Twentieth Amendment as originally ratified is:

> *Section 1—The terms of the President and Vice President shall end at noon on the 20th day of January, and the terms of Senators and Representatives at noon on the 3d day of January, of the years in which such terms would have ended if this article had not been ratified; and the terms of their successors shall then begin.*

> *Section 2—The Congress shall assemble at least once in every year, and such meeting shall begin at noon on the 3d day of January, unless they shall by law appoint a different day.*

Section 3—If, at the time fixed for the beginning of the term of the President, the President elect shall have died, the Vice President elect shall become President. If a President shall not have been chosen before the time fixed for the beginning of his term, or if the President elect shall have failed to qualify, then the Vice President elect shall act as President until a President shall have qualified; and the Congress may by law provide for the case wherein neither a President elect nor a Vice President elect shall have qualified, declaring who shall then act as President, or the manner in which one who is to act shall be selected, and such person shall act accordingly until a President or Vice President shall have qualified.

Section 4—The Congress may by law provide for the case of the death of any of the persons from whom the House of Representatives may choose a President whenever the right of choice shall have devolved upon them, and for the case of the death of any of the persons from whom the Senate may choose a Vice President whenever the right of choice shall have devolved upon them. Section 5—Sections 1 and 2 shall take effect on the 15th day of October following the ratification of this article. Section 6—This article shall be inoperative unless it shall have been ratified as an amendment to the Constitution by the legislatures of three-fourths of the several States within seven years from the date of its submission.

TWENTY-FIRST AMENDMENT

The Twenty-first Amendment (1933) to the Constitution of the United States officially repealed

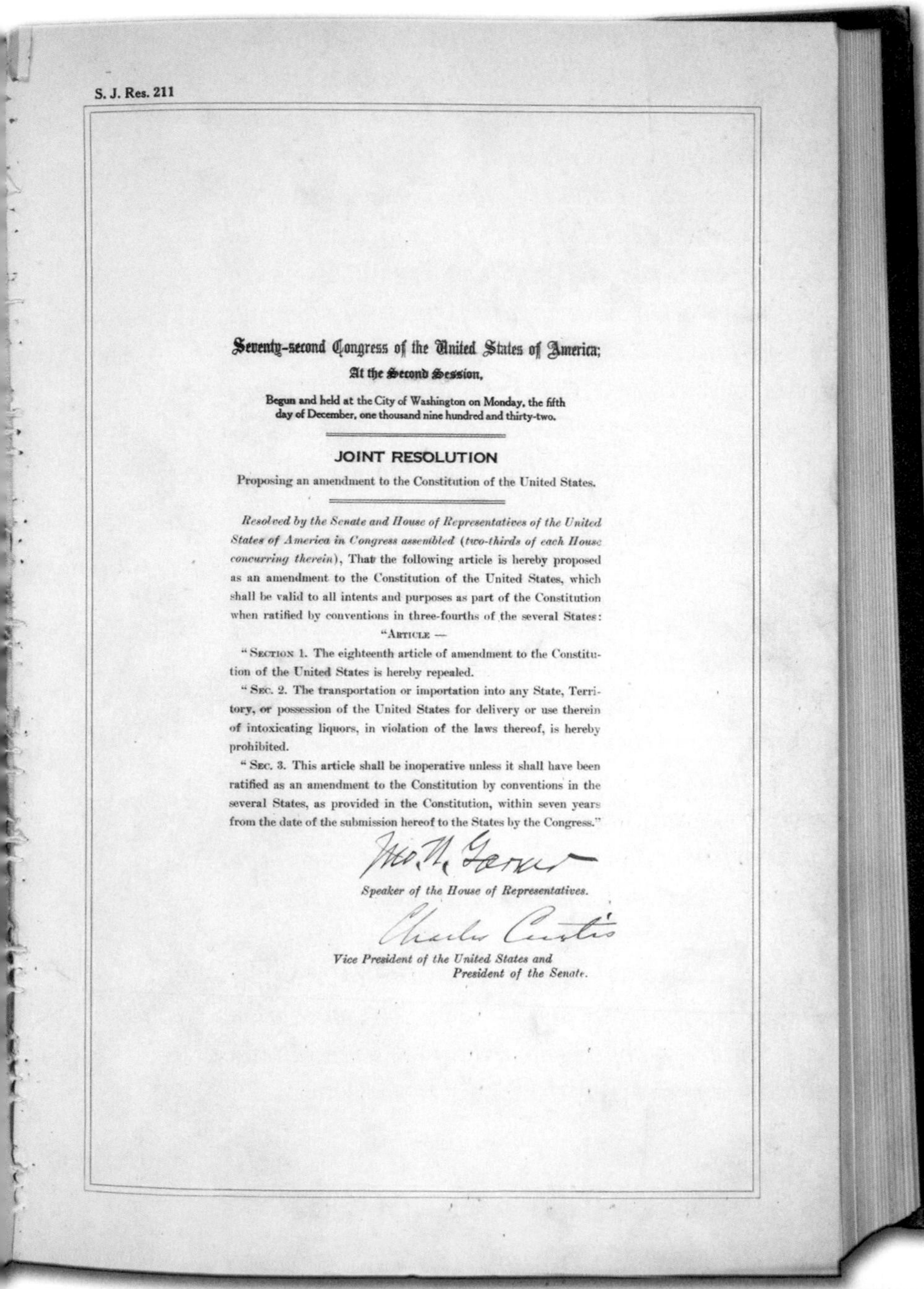

S. J. Res. 211

Seventy-second Congress of the United States of America;
At the Second Session,

Begun and held at the City of Washington on Monday, the fifth day of December, one thousand nine hundred and thirty-two.

JOINT RESOLUTION

Proposing an amendment to the Constitution of the United States.

Resolved by the Senate and House of Representatives of the United States of America in Congress assembled (two-thirds of each House concurring therein), That the following article is hereby proposed as an amendment to the Constitution of the United States, which shall be valid to all intents and purposes as part of the Constitution when ratified by conventions in three-fourths of the several States:

"ARTICLE —

"SECTION 1. The eighteenth article of amendment to the Constitution of the United States is hereby repealed.

"SEC. 2. The transportation or importation into any State, Territory, or possession of the United States for delivery or use therein of intoxicating liquors, in violation of the laws thereof, is hereby prohibited.

"SEC. 3. This article shall be inoperative unless it shall have been ratified as an amendment to the Constitution by conventions in the several States, as provided in the Constitution, within seven years from the date of the submission hereof to the States by the Congress."

Jno. N. Garner

Speaker of the House of Representatives.

Charles Curtis

Vice President of the United States and President of the Senate.

The Twenty-first Amendment to the Constitution of the United States, ratified in 1933. NARA

federal prohibition, which had been enacted through the Eighteenth Amendment, adopted in 1919. The Twenty-first Amendment is unique in two ways: (1) it is the only amendment that has repealed another amendment and (2) it is the only amendment that has used the auxiliary method of ratification via state conventions rather than the legislatures of the states.

The temperance movement was a strong force in U.S. politics in the early 20th century, enabling it to win passage of the Eighteenth Amendment. Its influence began to wane, however, in the wake of lax enforcement of Prohibition and the emerging illegal economies that quenched the thirst of many American adults. On Feb. 20, 1933, Congress proposed the Twenty-first Amendment, aimed at rescinding Prohibition, and in April Pres. Franklin D. Roosevelt signed the Cullen-Harrison Act, which amended the Prohibition-based Volstead Act to permit the manufacturing and sale of low-alcohol beer and wines. Ratification of the amendment was completed on Dec. 5, 1933.

While the public's attention focuses most often on the end of Prohibition, it is important to note that the Twenty-first Amendment also granted states greater leeway in regulating alcohol within and across their borders. Transportation and importation of alcohol could be regulated by the states as long as they did not violate the commerce clause of the Constitution.

The full text of the Twenty-first Amendment is:

> *Section 1—The eighteenth article of amendment to the Constitution of the United States is hereby repealed.*

> *Section 2—The transportation or importation into any State, Territory, or possession of the United States*

for delivery or use therein of intoxicating liquors, in violation of the laws thereof, is hereby prohibited.

Section 3—This article shall be inoperative unless it shall have been ratified as an amendment to the Constitution by conventions in the several States, as provided in the Constitution, within seven years from the date of the submission hereof to the States by the Congress.

TWENTY-SECOND AMENDMENT

The Twenty-second Amendment (1951) to the Constitution of the United States effectively limited to two the number of terms a president of the United States may serve.

The amendment was one of 273 recommendations to the U.S. Congress by the Hoover Commission, created by Pres. Harry S. Truman, to reorganize and reform the federal government. It was formally proposed by the U.S. Congress on March 24, 1947, and was ratified on Feb. 27, 1951.

The Constitution did not stipulate any limit on the number of presidential terms—indeed, as Alexander Hamilton wrote in Federalist 69: "That magistrate is to be elected for four years; and is to be re-eligible as often as the people of the United States shall think him worthy of their confidence." (Hamilton also argued, in Federalist 71, in favour of a life term for the president of the United States.) George Washington, the country's first president, opted to retire after two terms, setting a de facto informal "law" that was respected by the country's first 31 presidents that there should be rotation in office after two terms for the office of the presidency.

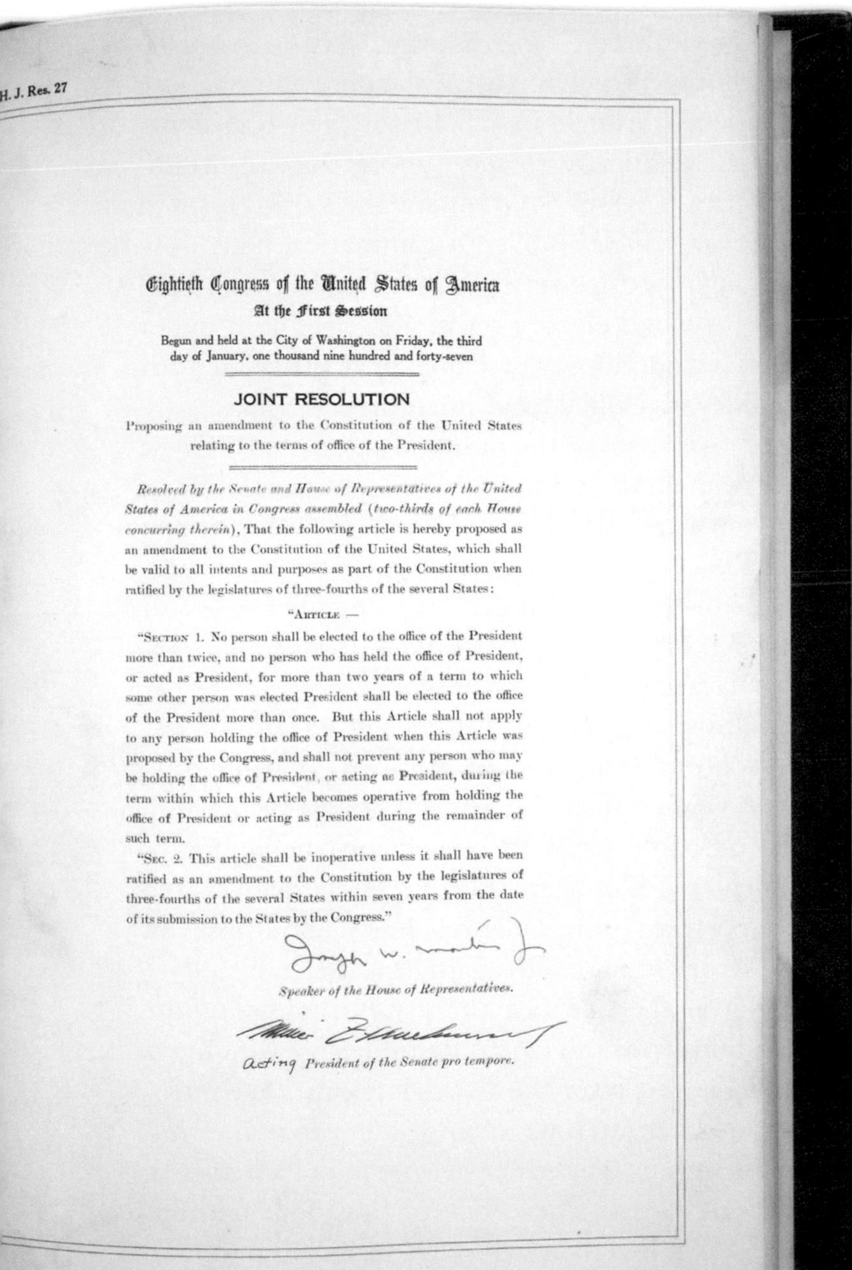
H. J. Res. 27

Eightieth Congress of the United States of America
At the First Session

Begun and held at the City of Washington on Friday, the third day of January, one thousand nine hundred and forty-seven

JOINT RESOLUTION

Proposing an amendment to the Constitution of the United States relating to the terms of office of the President.

Resolved by the Senate and House of Representatives of the United States of America in Congress assembled (two-thirds of each House concurring therein), That the following article is hereby proposed as an amendment to the Constitution of the United States, which shall be valid to all intents and purposes as part of the Constitution when ratified by the legislatures of three-fourths of the several States:

"ARTICLE —

"SECTION 1. No person shall be elected to the office of the President more than twice, and no person who has held the office of President, or acted as President, for more than two years of a term to which some other person was elected President shall be elected to the office of the President more than once. But this Article shall not apply to any person holding the office of President when this Article was proposed by the Congress, and shall not prevent any person who may be holding the office of President, or acting as President, during the term within which this Article becomes operative from holding the office of President or acting as President during the remainder of such term.

"SEC. 2. This article shall be inoperative unless it shall have been ratified as an amendment to the Constitution by the legislatures of three-fourths of the several States within seven years from the date of its submission to the States by the Congress."

Speaker of the House of Representatives.

acting *President of the Senate pro tempore.*

The Twenty-second Amendment to the Constitution of the United States, ratified in 1951. NARA

There is no clear indication that the decision to pursue the amendment was triggered by any single event or abuse of power. Indeed, throughout U.S. history, few presidents ever expressed the desire to serve more than the traditional two terms. Ulysses S. Grant sought a third term in 1880, but he was denied his party's nomination. Theodore Roosevelt sought a third term in 1912 but lost (it would have been his second elected term; vice president under William McKinley, Roosevelt came into office in 1901 when McKinley was killed by an anarchist).

In the 1930s, however, the national and global context brought forth an interruption to this two-term precedent.

In the midst of the Great Depression, Democrat Franklin D. Roosevelt had won election in 1932 and reelection in 1936. In 1940, as Europe was engulfed in a war that threatened to draw in the United States and without a clear Democratic successor who could consolidate the New Deal, Roosevelt, who had earlier indicated misgivings about a third term, agreed to break Washington's precedent. A general disinclination to change leadership amid crisis probably weighed heavily on the minds of voters—much more so than the perceived deep-seated opposition to a third term for a president—and Roosevelt romped to victory in 1940 and again in 1944.

Following on the heels of the establishment of the Hoover Commission and with Republicans winning a majority in Congress after the 1946 elections, they introduced an amendment to limit the president to two terms. The amendment caps the service of a president at 10 years. If a person succeeds to the office of president without election and serves less than two years, he may run for two full terms; otherwise, a person succeeding to the office of president can serve no more than a single elected term. Although there have been some calls for repeal of the amendment because it disallows voters to democratically elect the president of their choice, it has proved uncontroversial over the years. Nevertheless, presidents who win a second term in office are often referred to as "lame ducks," and the race to succeed them often begins even before their inauguration to a second term.

The full text of the Twenty-second Amendment is:

> *Section 1—No person shall be elected to the office of the President more than twice, and no person who has held the office of President, or acted as President, for more than two years of a term to which some other person was elected President shall be elected to the office of the President more than once. But this Article shall not apply to any person holding the office of President when this Article was proposed by the Congress, and shall not prevent any person who may be holding the office of President, or acting as President, during the term within which this Article becomes operative from holding the office of President or acting as President during the remainder of such term.*

> *Section 2—This article shall be inoperative unless it shall have been ratified as an amendment to the Constitution by the legislatures of three-fourths of the several States within seven years from the date of its submission to the States by the Congress.*

TWENTY-THIRD AMENDMENT

The Twenty-third Amendment (1961) to the Constitution of the United States granted citizens of Washington, D.C., the right to choose electors in

S. J. Res. 39

Eighty-sixth Congress of the United States of America

AT THE SECOND SESSION

Begun and held at the City of Washington on Wednesday, the sixth day of January, one thousand nine hundred and sixty

Joint Resolution

Proposing an amendment to the Constitution of the United States granting representation in the electoral college to the District of Columbia.

Resolved by the Senate and House of Representatives of the United States of America in Congress assembled (two-thirds of each House concurring therein), That the following article is hereby proposed as an amendment to the Constitution of the United States, which shall be valid to all intents and purposes as part of the Constitution only if ratified by the legislatures of three-fourths of the several States within seven years from the date of its submission by the Congress:

"ARTICLE —

"SECTION 1. The District constituting the seat of Government of the United States shall appoint in such manner as the Congress may direct:

"A number of electors of President and Vice President equal to the whole number of Senators and Representatives in Congress to which the District would be entitled if it were a State, but in no event more than the least populous State; they shall be in addition to those appointed by the States, but they shall be considered, for the purposes of the election of President and Vice President, to be electors appointed by a State; and they shall meet in the District and perform such duties as provided by the twelfth article of amendment.

"SEC. 2. The Congress shall have power to enforce this article by appropriate legislation".

Speaker of the House of Representatives.

~~*Vice President of the United States and*~~
Acting *President of the Senate.* pro tempore

The Twenty-third Amendment to the Constitution of the United States, ratified in 1961. NARA

presidential elections. The amendment was proposed by the U.S. Congress on June 16, 1960, and its ratification was certified on March 29, 1961. Washington is a federal district rather than a state, and residents of the District of Columbia are thus not citizens of a state. As such, though residents of the U.S. capital pay federal taxes and are subject to the same military obligations as citizens in the states, they historically have been denied the privilege of electing federal public officials. The Twenty-third Amendment established a vote for District residents in presidential elections, allocating to Washington electoral votes equal to the number of the least-populated state (in effect, three). Residents continue to be unrepresented in the U.S. Congress, though in 1970 Congress—which, according to the U.S. Constitution, has exclusive jurisdiction over the federal district—established a nonvoting elected delegate to the House of Representatives. Several "DC Statehood" organizations seeking to provide to the citizens of the District the full rights belonging to the citizens of any state have been established.

The full text of the Twenty-third Amendment is:

> *Section 1—The District constituting the seat of Government of the United States shall appoint in such manner as the Congress may direct: A number of electors of President and Vice President equal to the whole number of Senators and Representatives in Congress to which the District would be entitled if it were a State, but in no event more than the least populous State; they shall be in addition to those appointed by the States, but they shall be considered, for the purposes of the election of President and Vice President, to be electors appointed by a State; and they shall meet in the District and perform such duties as provided by the twelfth article of amendment.*

Section 2—The Congress shall have power to enforce this article by appropriate legislation.

TWENTY-FOURTH AMENDMENT

The Twenty-fourth Amendment (1964) to the Constitution of the United States prohibited the federal and state governments from requiring citizens to pay poll taxes as a condition of participation in a federal election. The amendment was proposed by the U.S. Congress on Aug. 27, 1962, and was ratified by the states on Jan. 23, 1964.

In 1870, following the American Civil War, the Fifteenth Amendment, guaranteeing the right to vote to former slaves, was adopted. The Twenty-fourth Amendment was adopted as a response to policies adopted in various Southern states after the ending of post-Civil War Reconstruction (1865–77) to limit the political participation of African-Americans. Such policies were bolstered by the 1937 U.S. Supreme Court decision in *Breedlove* v. *Suttles*, which upheld a Georgia poll tax. The Supreme Court reasoned that voting rights are conferred by the states and that the states may determine voter eligibility as they see fit, save for conflicts with the Fifteenth Amendment (respecting race) and the Nineteenth Amendment (respecting sex). It further ruled that a tax on voting did not amount to a violation of privileges or immunities protected by the Fourteenth Amendment. In short, because the tax applied to all voters—rather than just certain classes of voters—it did not violate the Fourteenth or Fifteenth Amendment.

During the civil rights era of the 1950s, particularly following the *Brown* v. *Board of Education* decision in 1954, such policies increasingly were seen as barriers to voting rights, particularly for African-Americans and the poor.

S. J. Res. 29

Eighty-seventh Congress of the United States of America

AT THE SECOND SESSION

Begun and held at the City of Washington on Wednesday, the tenth day of January, one thousand nine hundred and sixty-two

Joint Resolution

Proposing an amendment to the Constitution of the United States relating to the qualifications of electors.

Resolved by the Senate and House of Representatives of the United States of America in Congress assembled, That the following article is hereby proposed as an amendment to the Constitution of the United States, which shall be valid to all intents and purposes as part of the Constitution only if ratified by the legislatures of three-fourths of the several States within seven years from the date of its submission by the Congress:

"Article

"Section 1. The right of citizens of the United States to vote in any primary or other election for President or Vice President, for electors for President or Vice President, or for Senator or Representative in Congress, shall not be denied or abridged by the United States or any State by reason of failure to pay any poll tax or other tax.

"Sec. 2. The Congress shall have power to enforce this article by appropriate legislation."

John W. McCormack

Speaker of the House of Representatives.

Carl Hayden

~~*Vice President of the United States and*~~
President of the Senate pro tempore

The Twenty-fourth Amendment to the Constitution of the United States, ratified in 1964. NARA

Thus, the Twenty-fourth Amendment was proposed and ratified to eliminate an economic instrument that was used to limit voter participation. In *Harper* v. *Virginia Board of Electors* (1966), the U.S. Supreme Court, invoking the Fourteenth Amendment's equal protection clause, extended the prohibition of poll taxes to state elections.

The full text of the Twenty-fourth Amendment is:

> *Section 1—The right of citizens of the United States to vote in any primary or other election for President or Vice President, for electors for President or Vice President, or for Senator or Representative in Congress, shall not be denied or abridged by the United States or any State by reason of failure to pay any poll tax or other tax.*
>
> *Section 2—The Congress shall have power to enforce this article by appropriate legislation.*

TWENTY-FIFTH AMENDMENT

The Twenty-fifth Amendment (1967) to the Constitution of the United States set forth succession rules relating to vacancies and disabilities for the offices of the president and vice president. The amendment was proposed by the U.S. Congress on July 6, 1965, and it was ratified on Feb. 10, 1967.

While the first section of the Twenty-fifth Amendment codified the traditionally observed process of succession in the event of the death of the president—that the vice president would succeed to the office—it also introduced a change regarding the ascent of the vice president to president should the latter resign from office. In the event of resignation, the vice president would assume the title and position of president—not acting president—effectively prohibiting the departing president from returning to office.

The second section of the amendment addresses vacancies in the office of the vice president. Traditionally, when the office of vice president was vacant, usually through the vice president's succession to the presidency following the death of the president, the office of vice president stood vacant until the next election. Through the Twenty-fifth Amendment, the president would nominate a vice president, who would be subject to confirmation by the U.S. Congress. Only a few years after the amendment's ratification, this section was put into effect. In 1973 Spiro Agnew resigned as Pres. Richard M. Nixon's vice president, and Nixon subsequently selected Gerald R. Ford, who was then serving as minority leader in the House of Representatives, to serve as vice president. Despite the fact that Nixon and Ford were Republicans and the Democrats retained majorities in both the House and the Senate, Ford was easily confirmed, which indicated that the process would focus less on policy positions than on general fitness for office. Ford assumed the duties of vice president on Dec. 6, 1973, and upon Nixon's resignation from office to avoid impeachment, Ford became the first president to accede to office according to the Twenty-fifth Amendment on Aug. 9, 1974. Had the Twenty-fifth Amendment not been in effect, Nixon would not have been able to replace Agnew, and it remains a matter of speculation whether Nixon would have resigned prior to impeachment and a trial and thus enabled the Democratic speaker of the House of Representatives to become president under the Presidential Succession Act of 1947.

The third section of the amendment sets forth the formal process for determining the capacity of the president to discharge the powers and duties of office. It assumes that the president has the presence of mind and physical

S. J. Res. 1

Eighty-ninth Congress of the United States of America

AT THE FIRST SESSION

Begun and held at the City of Washington on Monday, the fourth day of January, one thousand nine hundred and sixty-five

Joint Resolution

Proposing an amendment to the Constitution of the United States relating to succession to the Presidency and Vice Presidency and to cases where the President is unable to discharge the powers and duties of his office.

Resolved by the Senate and House of Representatives of the United States of America in Congress assembled (two-thirds of each House concurring therein), That the following article is proposed as an amendment to the Constitution of the United States, which shall be valid to all intents and purposes as part of the Constitution when ratified by the legislatures of three-fourths of the several States within seven years from the date of its submission by the Congress:

"ARTICLE —

"SECTION 1. In case of the removal of the President from office or of his death or resignation, the Vice President shall become President.

"SEC. 2. Whenever there is a vacancy in the office of the Vice President, the President shall nominate a Vice President who shall take office upon confirmation by a majority vote of both Houses of Congress.

"SEC. 3. Whenever the President transmits to the President pro tempore of the Senate and the Speaker of the House of Representatives his written declaration that he is unable to discharge the powers and duties of his office, and until he transmits to them a written declaration to the contrary, such powers and duties shall be discharged by the Vice President as Acting President.

"SEC. 4. Whenever the Vice President and a majority of either the principal officers of the executive departments or of such other body as Congress may by law provide, transmit to the President pro tempore of the Senate and the Speaker of the House of Representatives their written declaration that the President is unable to discharge the powers and duties of his office, the Vice President shall immediately assume the powers and duties of the office as Acting President.

"Thereafter, when the President transmits to the President pro tempore of the Senate and the Speaker of the House of Representatives his written declaration that no inability exists, he shall resume the powers and duties of his office unless the Vice President and a majority of either the principal officers of the executive department or of such other body as Congress may by law provide, transmit within four days to the President pro tempore of the Senate and the Speaker of the House of Representatives their written declaration that the President is unable to discharge the powers and duties of his office. Thereupon Congress shall decide the issue, assembling within forty-eight hours for that purpose if not in session. If the Congress, within

The first page of the Twenty-fifth Amendment to the Constitution of the United States, ratified in 1967. NARA

S. J. Res. 1—2

twenty-one days after receipt of the latter written declaration, or, if Congress is not in session, within twenty-one days after Congress is required to assemble, determines by two-thirds vote of both Houses that the President is unable to discharge the powers and duties of his office, the Vice President shall continue to discharge the same as Acting President; otherwise, the President shall resume the powers and duties of his office."

Speaker of the House of Representatives.

Vice President of the United States and
President of the Senate.

The second page of the Twenty-fifth Amendment to the Constitution of the United States, ratified in 1967. NARA

ability to produce a written statement formally notifying the president pro tempore of the Senate and the speaker of the House of such circumstances, which would result in the vice president's temporarily serving as acting president. In the event that a president may be unable to declare his inability to discharge the powers and duties of office, the fourth section of the amendment requires such determinations to be made jointly by the vice president and the cabinet, with the vice president immediately assuming the position of acting president.

Prior to the passage of the amendment, nine presidents—William Henry Harrison, Zachary Taylor, Abraham Lincoln, James Garfield, William McKinley, Woodrow Wilson, Warren G. Harding, Franklin D. Roosevelt, and Dwight D. Eisenhower—experienced health crises that left them temporarily incapacitated, with death resulting in six cases (Harrison, Taylor, Lincoln, Garfield, McKinley, and Harding). After the passage of the amendment, Pres. Ronald Reagan was incapacitated for some 24 hours while undergoing surgery for a gunshot wound resulting from a failed assassination attempt, though no official designation of presidential responsibility was ever made. Indeed, this portion of the Twenty-fifth Amendment has never been invoked.

The full text of the Twenty-fifth Amendment is:

> *Section 1—In case of the removal of the President from office or of his death or resignation, the Vice President shall become President.*

> *Section 2—Whenever there is a vacancy in the office of the Vice President, the President shall nominate a Vice President who shall take office upon confirmation by a majority vote of both Houses of Congress.*

Section 3—Whenever the President transmits to the President pro tempore of the Senate and the Speaker of the House of Representatives his written declaration that he is unable to discharge the powers and duties of his office, and until he transmits to them a written declaration to the contrary, such powers and duties shall be discharged by the Vice President as Acting President.

Section 4—Whenever the Vice President and a majority of either the principal officers of the executive departments or of such other body as Congress may by law provide, transmit to the President pro tempore of the Senate and the Speaker of the House of Representatives their written declaration that the President is unable to discharge the powers and duties of his office, the Vice President shall immediately assume the powers and duties of the office as Acting President.

Thereafter, when the President transmits to the President pro tempore of the Senate and the Speaker of the House of Representatives his written declaration that no inability exists, he shall resume the powers and duties of his office unless the Vice President and a majority of either the principal officers of the executive department or of such other body as Congress may by law provide, transmit within four days to the President pro tempore of the Senate and the Speaker of the House of Representatives their written declaration that the President is unable to discharge the powers and duties of his office. Thereupon Congress shall decide the issue, assembling within forty-eight hours for that purpose if not in session. If the Congress, within twenty-one days after receipt of the latter written declaration, or, if Congress is not in session, within twenty-one days after Congress is required to assemble, determines by two-thirds vote of both Houses that the President is unable to discharge the powers and duties of his office, the Vice President shall continue to discharge the same as Acting President; otherwise, the President shall resume the powers and duties of his office.

TWENTY-SIXTH AMENDMENT

The Twenty-sixth Amendment (1971) to the Constitution of the United States extended voting rights to citizens aged 18 or older.

Traditionally, the voting age in most states was 21, though in the 1950s Pres. Dwight D. Eisenhower signaled support for lowering it. Attempts at establishing a national standardized voting age, however, were met with opposition from the states. In 1970 Pres. Richard M. Nixon signed an extension of the Voting Rights Act, which lowered the age of eligibility to vote in all federal and state elections to 18. (Nixon himself was skeptical of the constitutionality of this provision.) Two states (Oregon and Texas) filed suit, claiming that the law violated the reserve powers of the states to set their own voting-age requirements, and in *Oregon* v. *Mitchell* (1970) the Supreme Court upheld this claim.

In response to this setback, and spurred by student activism during the Vietnam War and the fact that 18-year-olds could be drafted to fight in the war but could not vote in federal elections in most states, an amendment

S. J. Res. 7

Ninety-second Congress of the United States of America

AT THE FIRST SESSION

Begun and held at the City of Washington on Thursday, the twenty-first day of January, one thousand nine hundred and seventy-one

Joint Resolution

Proposing an amendment to the Constitution of the United States extending the right to vote to citizens eighteen years of age or older.

Resolved by the Senate and House of Representatives of the United States of America in Congress assembled (two-thirds of each House concurring therein), That the following article is proposed as an amendment to the Constitution of the United States, which shall be valid to all intents and purposes as part of the Constitution when ratified by the legislatures of three-fourths of the several States within seven years from the date of its submission by the Congress:

"Article —

"Section 1. The right of citizens of the United States, who are eighteen years of age or older, to vote shall not be denied or abridged by the United States or by any State on account of age.

"Sec. 2. The Congress shall have power to enforce this article by appropriate legislation."

Carl Albert
Speaker of the House of Representatives.

Allen J. Ellender
~~Vice President of the United States and~~
President of the Senate. Pro Tempore

The Twenty-sixth Amendment to the Constitution of the United States, ratified in 1971. NARA

was introduced in the U.S. Congress. It won congressional backing on March 23, 1971, and it was ratified by the states on July 1, 1971—the quickest time in which a proposed amendment had been ratified. The administrator of general services officially certified ratification of the Twenty-sixth Amendment on July 7.

The full text of the Twenty-sixth Amendment is:

> *Section 1—The right of citizens of the United States, who are eighteen years of age or older, to vote shall not be denied or abridged by the United States or by any State on account of age.*
>
> *Section 2—The Congress shall have power to enforce this article by appropriate legislation.*

TWENTY-SEVENTH AMENDMENT

The Twenty-seventh Amendment (1992) to the Constitution of the United States required that any change to the rate of compensation for members of the U.S. Congress take effect only after the next election of the House of Representatives.

Commonly known as the Congressional Compensation Act of 1789, the Twenty-seventh Amendment was actually the second of 12 amendments proposed by the first Congress in 1789 (10 of these would be ratified and become the Bill of Rights). Absent a time period for ratification by the states, the expiration of which would render the amendment inoperable, it remained dormant for almost 80 years after only six states voted for ratification (Delaware, Maryland, North Carolina, South Carolina, Vermont, and Virginia). In

ARCHIVIST OF THE UNITED STATES
UNITED STATES OF AMERICA

TO ALL TO WHOM THESE PRESENTS SHALL COME,

GREETING:

KNOW YE, That the first Congress of the United States, at its first session, held in New York, New York, on the twenty-fifth day of September, in the year one thousand seven hundred and eighty-nine, passed the following resolution to amend the Constitution of the United States of America, in the following words and figures in part, to wit:

> *The Conventions of a number of the States having at the time of their adopting the Constitution, expressed a desire, in order to prevent misconstruction or abuse of its powers, that further declaratory and restrictive clauses should be added: And as extending the ground of public confidence in the Government will best ensure the benificent ends of its institution;*
>
> *Resolved by the Senate and House of Representatives of the United States of America in Congress assembled, two thirds of both Houses concurring, that the following Articles be proposed to the Legislatures of the several States, as Amendments to the Constitution of the United States, all or any of which Articles, when ratified by three fourths of the said Legislatures, to be valid to all intents and purposes, as part of the said Constitution, viz.:*

The first page of the Twenty-seventh Amendment to the Constitution of the United States, ratified in 1992. NARA

Articles in addition to, and amendment of, the Constitution of the United States of America, proposed by Congress and ratified by the Legislatures of the several States, pursuant to the fifth Article of the original Constitution.

* * * * * * *

Article the Second...No law, varying the compensation for the services of the Senators and Representatives, shall take effect, until an election of Representatives shall have intervened.

* * * * * * *

And, further, that Section 106b, Title 1 of the United States Code provides that whenever official notice is received at the National Archives and Records Administration that any amendment proposed to the Constitution of the United States has been adopted, according to the provisions of the Constitution, the Archivist of the United States shall forthwith cause the amendment to be published, with his certificate, specifying the States by which the same may have been adopted, and that the same has become valid, to all intents and purposes, as a part of the Constitution of the United States.

And, further, that it appears from official documents on file in the National Archives of the United States that the Amendment to the Constitution of the United States proposed as aforesaid has been ratified by the Legislatures of the States of Alabama, Alaska, Arizona, Arkansas, Colorado, Connecticut, Delaware, Florida, Georgia, Idaho, Illinois, Indiana, Iowa, Kansas, Louisiana, Maine, Maryland, Michigan, Minnesota, Missouri, Montana, Nevada, New Hampshire, New Jersey, New Mexico, North Carolina, North Dakota, Ohio, Oklahoma, Oregon, South Carolina, South Dakota, Tennessee, Texas, Utah, Vermont, Virginia, West Virginia, Wisconsin, and Wyoming.

The second page of the Twenty-seventh Amendment to the Constitution of the United States, ratified in 1992. NARA

And, further, that the States whose Legislatures have so ratified the said proposed Amendment constitute the requisite three fourths of the whole number of States in the United States.

NOW, Therefore, be it known that I, Don W. Wilson, Archivist of the United States, by virtue and in pursuance of Section 106b, Title 1 of the United States Code, do hereby certify that the aforesaid Amendment has b[illegible]id, to all intents and purposes, as a part of the Constitution of [illegible]e United [illegible]es.

IN TESTIMONY WHEREOF,
I have hereunto set my hand and caused the seal of the National Archives and Records Administration to be affixed.

DONE at the City of Washington this 18th day of May in the year of our Lord one thousand nine hundred and ninety-two.

[signature]

DON W. WILSON

[illegible]oregoing was signed [illegible]y presence on this 18 day of [illegible], 1992.

Martha L. G[illegible]

The third page of the Twenty-seventh Amendment to the Constitution of the United States, ratified in 1992. NARA

1873 Ohio ratified the amendment as an expression of dissatisfaction with then-current attempts by Congress to increase the salaries of its members. The amendment once again lay dormant, but in 1978 another state, Wyoming, ratified it. In 1982, after an undergraduate research paper written by Gregory Watson, then a student at the University of Texas in Austin, became the foundation for a movement to curtail political corruption by ratifying the amendment, efforts picked up steam. (Watson had received a "C" for the paper, his professor saying that the argument that the amendment was still pending was not convincing.) By May 5, 1992, the requisite 38 states had ratified the amendment (North Carolina had re-ratified it in 1989), and it was certified by the archivist of the United States as the Twenty-seventh Amendment on May 18, 1992, more than 202 years after its original proposal.

The full text of the Twenty-seventh Amendment is:

> *No law, varying the compensation for the services of the Senators and Representatives, shall take effect, until an election of Representatives shall have intervened.*

CHAPTER 4

Constitutional Law

Constitutional law comprises the body of rules, doctrines, and practices that govern the operation of political communities. The term also refers to the branch of legal study that concerns such rules, doctrines, and practices.

In modern times the most important political community has been the state. Modern constitutional law is the offspring of nationalism as well as of the idea that the state must protect certain fundamental rights of the individual. As the number of states has multiplied, so have constitutions and with them the body of constitutional law, though sometimes such law originates from sources outside the state. The protection of individual rights, meanwhile, has become the concern of supranational institutions, particularly since the mid-20th century.

THE NATURE OF CONSTITUTIONAL LAW

In the broadest sense, a constitution is a body of rules governing the affairs of an organized group. A parliament, a church congregation, a social club, or a trade union may operate under the terms of a formal written document labeled a constitution. Not all of the rules of the organization are in the constitution; many other rules (e.g., bylaws and customs) also exist. By definition the rules spelled out in the constitution are considered to be basic, in the sense that, until they are modified according to an appropriate procedure, all other rules must conform to them. Thus, the presiding officer of an organization may be obliged to declare a proposal out of order if it is contrary to a provision in the Constitution. Implicit in the concept of a constitution is the idea of a "higher law" that takes precedence over all other laws.

Every political community, and thus every state, has a constitution, at least insofar as it operates its important institutions according to some fundamental body of rules. By this conception of the term, the only conceivable alternative to a constitution is a condition of anarchy. Nevertheless, the form a constitution may take varies considerably. Constitutions may be written or unwritten, codified or uncodified, and complex or simple, and they may provide for vastly different patterns of governance. In a constitutional monarchy, for example, the sovereign's powers are circumscribed by the constitution, whereas in an absolute monarchy the sovereign has unqualified powers.

A political community's constitution articulates the principles determining the institutions to which the task of governing is entrusted, along with their respective powers. In absolute monarchies, as in the ancient kingdoms of East Asia, the Roman Empire, and France between the 16th and 18th centuries, all sovereign powers were concentrated in one person, the king or emperor, who exercised them directly or through subordinate agencies that acted according to his instructions. In ancient republics, such as Athens and Rome, the constitution provided, as do the constitutions of most modern states, for a distribution of powers among distinct institutions. But whether it concentrates or disperses these powers, a constitution always contains at least the rules that define the structure and operation of the government that runs the community.

A constitution may do more than define the authorities endowed with powers to command. It may also delimit those powers in order to secure against them certain fundamental rights of persons or groups. The idea that there should be limits on the powers that the state may exercise is deeply rooted in Western political philosophy. Well before the advent of Christianity, Greek philosophers thought that, in order to be just, positive law—the law actually enforced in a community—must reflect the principles of a superior, ideal law, which was known as natural law. Similar conceptions were propagated in Rome by Cicero (106–43 BCE) and by the Stoics. Later the Church Fathers and the theologians of Scholasticism held that positive law is binding only if it does not conflict with the precepts of divine law. These abstract considerations were received to a certain extent in the fundamental rules of positive legal systems. In Europe during the Middle Ages, for example, the authority of political rulers did not extend to religious matters, which were strictly reserved to the jurisdiction of the church. Their powers also were limited by the rights granted to at least some classes of subjects. Disputes over the extent of such rights were not infrequent and sometimes were settled through solemn legal "pacts" between the contenders, such as Magna Carta (1215). Even the "absolute" monarchs of Europe did not always exercise genuinely absolute power. The king of France in the 17th or 18th century, for example, was unable by himself to alter the fundamental laws of the kingdom or to disestablish the Roman Catholic Church.

Against this background of existing legal limitations on the powers of governments, a decisive turn in the history of Western constitutional law occurred when political philosophers developed a theory of natural law based on the "inalienable rights" of the individual. The English philosopher John Locke (1632–1704) was an early champion of this doctrine. Others followed Locke, and in the 18th century the view they articulated became the banner of the Enlightenment. These thinkers asserted that every human being is endowed with certain rights—including the rights to worship according to one's conscience, to express one's opinions in public, to acquire and possess property, and to be protected against punishment on the basis of retroactive laws and unfair criminal procedures—that governments cannot "take away" because they are not created by governments in the first place. They further assumed that governments should be organized in a way that affords effective protection for individual rights. Thus, it was thought that, as a minimal prerequisite, governmental functions must be divided into legislative, executive, and judicial; executive action must comply with the rules laid down by the legislature; and remedies, administered by an independent judiciary, must be available against illegal executive action.

The doctrine of natural rights was a potent factor in the reshaping of the constitutions of Western countries in the 17th, 18th, and 19th centuries. An early stage of this process was the creation of the English Bill of Rights (1689), a product of England's Glorious Revolution. All these principles concerning the division of governmental functions and their appropriate relations were incorporated into the constitutional law of England and other Western countries. England also soon changed some of its laws so as to give more-adequate legal force to the newly pronounced individual freedoms.

In the United States the doctrine of natural rights was even more successful. Once the American colonies became independent states (1776), they faced the problem of giving themselves a fresh political organization. They seized the opportunity to spell out in legal documents, which could be amended only through a special procedure, the main principles for distributing governmental functions among distinct state agencies and for protecting the rights of the individual, as the doctrine of natural rights required. The federal Constitution—drafted in 1787 at a Constitutional

John Locke, English philosopher whose pioneering works of modern thought inspired both the European Enlightenment and the U.S. Constitution, as painted by Sir Godfrey Kneller. Locke believed that people naturally possess certain rights, chief among them life, liberty, and property. Rulers, he said, derived their power only from the consent of the people. The Bridgeman Art Library/Getty Images

Convention in Philadelphia to replace the failing Articles of Confederation—and its subsequent Bill of Rights (ratified 1791) did the same at the national level. By formally conferring through these devices a higher status on rules that defined the organization of government and limited its legislative and executive powers, U.S. constitutionalism displayed the essential nature of all constitutional law: the fact that it is "basic" with respect to all other laws of the legal system. This feature made it possible to establish institutional controls over the conformity of legislation with the group of rules considered, within the system, to be of supreme importance.

The American idea that the basic rules that guide the operations of government should be stated in an orderly, comprehensive document quickly became popular. From the end of the 18th century, scores of countries in Europe and elsewhere followed the example of the United States; today nearly all states have constitutional documents describing the fundamental organs of the state, the ways they should operate, and, usually, the rights they must respect and even sometimes the goals they ought to pursue. Not every constitution, however, has been inspired by the individualistic ideals that permeate modern Western constitutional law. The constitutions of the former Soviet Union and other communist countries subordinated individual freedoms to the goal of achieving a classless society. Notwithstanding the great differences between modern constitutions, however, they are similar at least in one respect: they are meant to express the core of the constitutional law governing their respective countries.

CHARACTERISTICS OF CONSTITUTIONS

It is often asserted that the United States has a written constitution and the United Kingdom an unwritten one. In one sense this is true: in the United States there is a formal document called the Constitution, whereas there is no such document in the United Kingdom. In fact, however, many parts of the British constitution exist in written form; for this reason, most scholars prefer to classify it as "uncodified" rather than unwritten. Moreover, there are important aspects of the U.S. Constitution that are wholly unwritten. The British constitution includes, for example, the Bill of Rights (1689), the Act of Settlement (1701), the Parliament Act of 1911, the successive Representation of the People Acts (which extended suffrage), the statutes dealing with the structure of the courts, and various local government acts. On the other hand, certain institutions of constitutional significance in the United States, including the system of political parties and judicial review of legislative and executive actions, are not mentioned in the written U.S. Constitution. Indeed, written constitutions can never exhaust the whole constitutional law of a state. They are always supplemented, to varying degrees, by statutes, judicial doctrines interpreting the constitution, intergovernmental practices, and nongovernmental institutions (such as political parties) and their practices.

Whether long or short, written constitutions can concern themselves exclusively or prevalently with the organization of government or deal extensively also with the rights of the people and with the goals of governmental action. The U.S. Constitution, at roughly 7,000 words, is a model of brevity, and many constitutions in Western countries are only slightly longer. In contrast, the constitution of India extends to hundreds of pages. Merely "organizational" constitutions—documents containing no guarantees of rights or prescriptions of goals—are now rare. More recent written constitutions are generally longer and encompass a wider range of rights accorded to citizens.

Written constitutions are said to be "normative" when all their binding principles are observed, more or less, in

The U.S. Constitution has no language regarding the formation of political parties—such as the Democrats and Republicans—nor on that of political groups, such as the Tea Party, a conservative populist social and political movement. Here, Tea Party members protest on Apr. 15, 2009, at the Federal Building Plaza in Chicago, Ill., as part of a coast-to-coast demonstration on income tax day. Scott Olson/Getty Images

the actual operations of the political system. A constitution is considered "nominal" if it is largely or in substantial parts disregarded and does not provide insight into the real functioning of the political system. Normative constitutions predominate in the United States, Australia, Canada, Japan, and the countries of western Europe, while nominal constitutions are common in countries ruled by a one-person or a one-party dictatorship or by a military junta.

Constitutions also can be classified as "rigid" or "flexible." Those that are rigid stipulate that at least some part of the constitution cannot be modified by the same procedures used to enact statutory law. Those that are flexible allow any of the rules of the constitution to be modified through the simple procedure by which ordinary statutes are enacted. The U.S. Constitution is rigid, as an amendment requires supermajorities at both the proposal and ratification stages (the most common method of amendment is proposal by a two-thirds vote in both houses of Congress followed by ratification by three-fourths of the states). The United Kingdom's constitution is flexible, because any of its constitutional institutions and rules can be abrogated or modified by an act of Parliament. The great majority of countries have rigid constitutions.

Only under rigid constitutions is it possible to establish institutional controls to ensure the conformity of legislation with the principles considered indispensable for the well-being of the community. Nevertheless, a rigid constitution does not by itself guarantee the stability and continuity of a country's constitutional law. Although the amending process in the United States is difficult, it is easier than the process in other countries with rigid constitutions. In Switzerland, for example, amendments to the federal constitution of 1874 are proposed by the legislature or by a petition of 100,000 citizens and require for their approval a majority vote in a national referendum and ratification by a majority of voters in each of a majority of the cantons. (The Swiss Confederation is comprised of 23 such political subdivisions.) Nevertheless, the provisions of the Swiss constitution have been changed repeatedly on many important points. In addition, even if the provisions of a rigid constitution remain unaltered, they often assume over time different meaning and scope because formal constitutional provisions are subject to interpretation by the courts or by the legislature, the executive, and other institutional subjects. Thus, the commerce and due process clauses of the U.S. Constitution do not have the same legal implications today as they did in the 19th century. To a certain extent interpretation inevitably involves adaptation of the letter of the law to societal changes.

Constitutional law in countries with flexible constitutions does not have to be unstable or constantly in flux. The United Kingdom can modify its constitutional law by statute (or even in important areas by "conventions" between the supreme institutional powers of the state: the crown, Parliament, and the cabinet). Nevertheless, statutes and common-law principles of constitutional import cannot be changed as easily as other statutes and rules and are generally treated as permanent. Thus, the principle of the "rule of law"—roughly the equivalent of the American due process principle—has been an essential element of the British constitution since approximately the late 17th century. This continuity has been ensured by a broad consensus between the crown, political leaders, and citizens that such principles are crucial to the country's constitution—not by the existence of any institutional obstacles to changing them.

Thus, the relative continuity of a country's constitutional law does not depend entirely on the adoption of a rigid constitution, though such a constitution may make changes at times more complicated and difficult. It depends rather on the people's attitude concerning the fundamental political values the legal system ought to honour. If and when this attitude changes, the new viewpoint is likely to eventually make its way into the constitution, whether through the amending process and interpretation by the courts under a rigid constitution or through easier legislative procedures under a flexible constitution. (Of course, there exists the further possibility of change, in both cases, through the extreme means of a popular revolution or a military coup d'état.) Because the political values felt to be supreme by the dominant forces in a community have ultimate controlling influence, some European continental scholars have been prompted to call them the "material constitution," at any given historical moment, of that community. The development of the material constitution is decisive in determining the retention or demise—as well as the actual meaning and scope in application—of the principles and rules of the written constitution, whether the latter is rigid or flexible.

UNITARY AND FEDERAL SYSTEMS

No modern country can be governed from a single location only. The affairs of municipalities and rural areas must be left to the administration of local governments. Accordingly, all countries have at least two levels of government: central and local. A number of countries also contain a third level of government, which is responsible for the interests of more or less large regions.

The distribution of powers between different levels of government is an important aspect of the constitutional organization of a state. Among states with two levels of government, distinctions can be made on the basis of the greater or lesser autonomy granted to the local level. The British government's respect for local self-government has always been a characteristic of its constitution. In contrast, France traditionally had kept its local authorities under strict central control. In countries with three levels of government, the distribution of powers between the central and the intermediate governments varies. States formed through the union of formerly independent states usually maintain an intermediate level with considerable legislative, executive, and judicial powers (as in the United States, Argentina, and Switzerland), though some grant few powers to this level. The latter situation occurs often in countries that have introduced the intermediate level as a correction to their previous choice of two levels—as Italy did in its constitution of 1948 and Spain in its constitution of 1978.

Depending on how a constitution organizes power between the central and subnational governments, a country may be said to possess either a unitary or a federal system. In a unitary system the only level of government besides the central is the local or municipal government. Although local governments may enjoy considerable autonomy, their powers are not accorded constitutional status; the central government determines which decisions to "devolve" to the local level and may abolish local governments if it so chooses. In federal systems there is an intermediate level of governmental authority between the central and the local; it usually consists of states or provinces, though other entities (e.g., cantons or republics) may exist in some countries. Aside from the number of levels, the most important distinction between a unitary system and a federal one is that the states or provinces of a federal state have constitutionally protected sovereignty.

Within a federal system the state or provincial governments share sovereignty with the central government and have final jurisdiction over a broad range of policy areas.

Federal and unitary systems are ideal types, representing the endpoints of a continuum. Most countries fall somewhere in between the two extremes—states can be more or less unitary or more or less federal. So-called "semifederal" countries occupy a middle category, possessing an intermediate level of government that does not have the same protections of sovereignty that the states or provinces of federal states enjoy.

A proper understanding of these types of constitution requires the consideration of additional features of each type. The model federal state is characterized by the existence, at the national level, of a written, rigid constitution guaranteeing the several intermediate governments not only permanence and independence but also a full complement of legislative, executive, and judicial powers. The national constitution enumerates the powers granted to the central government; the remaining powers are reserved to the intermediate governments at the state or provincial level. These subnational entities are generally represented at the national level, possibly on an equal footing, in a second chamber of the national legislature (often called the upper house, or senate). They also often are central to the process of amending the national constitution. For example, some number of state or provincial legislatures may be required to consent to the ratification of amendments passed by the federal legislature. States or provinces in federal systems also have their own constitutions that define the institutions of their respective governments, as well as the powers that are devolved further to their local governments. Such constitutional arrangements are a guarantee against possible efforts of the central government to enlarge its jurisdiction and so imperil the important political role that intermediate governments play in a federal system. More than formal constitutional safeguards are required to preserve that role. Apart from constitutional amendments, the central government may seek to broaden its own powers through the use of constitutional clauses granting "implied powers." In some federal states (e.g., Argentina and India), there are emergency provisions by which the central government may suspend the powers of individual state or provincial governments. If abused, these provisions—meant to be used only in cases of rebellion or other severe disturbance against the constitutional order—may seriously compromise the constitutionally enshrined principle of shared sovereignty that is the hallmark of federalism. Even in established federal democracies (e.g., Canada, Germany, and the United States), the exact distribution of powers between levels of government is a matter of constant dispute between central and subnational governments. Disputes about federal-state matters are often the subject of rulings in courts or constitutional tribunals or conferences involving the heads of the central and subnational governments.

Semifederal states are also based, as a rule, on rigid written constitutions granting some limited legislative and administrative (though seldom judicial) powers to the intermediate or regional governments. But because regional governments in semifederal states possess jurisdiction only over enumerated matters (and even here they are subject in part to the overriding powers of the central authorities), their actual role and political influence within the system largely depend on the tendency of the central government to buttress or to restrict their autonomy. Where the powers granted by the constitution to the regional governments are particularly minimal, the semifederal state will look in many respects like a unitary state.

DEVOLUTION

Devolution is the transfer of power from a central government to subnational (e.g., state, regional, or local) authorities. Devolution usually occurs through conventional statutes rather than through a change in a country's constitution; thus, unitary systems of government that have devolved powers in this manner are still considered unitary rather than federal systems because the powers of the subnational authorities can be withdrawn by the central government at any time. Throughout history, there has been a tendency for governments to centralize power. From the late 20th century, however, groups in both federal and unitary systems increasingly sought to reduce the power of central governments by devolving power to local or regional governments. For example, supporters of states' rights in the United States favoured diffusing power away from Washington, D.C., toward state and local governments. This trend was also experienced throughout the world, though perhaps the two most notable instances of devolution occurred in France in the 1980s and the United Kingdom in the late 1990s. Devolution is viewed in many countries as a way to dampen regional, racial, ethnic, or religious cleavages, particularly in multiethnic societies, such as Sri Lanka and Indonesia. Devolution has also occurred in Finland, where the government has granted significant autonomy to the largely Swedish-speaking population of the Åland Islands; in Spain, where regional governments (particularly the Basque Country, Catalonia, Galicia, and Andalusia) have enjoyed extensive powers; and in Italy, where several regions have been granted "special autonomy" by the central government.

Where the powers are relatively large and the central government favours their expansion—perhaps because the central government is itself a coalition of national and regional parties—the state tends to assume federal characteristics, even if the typical hallmarks of the federal system are not present. Spain and Belgium are good examples of semifederal states that have become increasingly more federal in practice.

FEDERAL AND SEMIFEDERAL STATES

Classifying a particular state as federal or unitary is usually straightforward, though in some cases it can be more difficult. The United States and Switzerland are clearly federal states; all of the above-mentioned characteristics of the federal state are present in their constitutional systems. Australia and Germany, too, can be considered federal in all respects. Canada also is a federal state, despite the fact that some of the formal features of ideal federalism are absent from its 1982 constitution: the provinces' powers, not the central government's, are enumerated. Additionally, there is no constitutionally mandated representation of the provinces in the upper house of the federal legislature, whose members are appointed by the central government (though they are chosen, by convention, in a way that ensures provincial representation). Nevertheless, the provinces' powers are vast, and the constitutional guarantees of their rights and independence are particularly strong.

There are several federal states in Latin America. Argentina and Brazil probably are the most clearly federal, with rigid constitutions, equal representation of the regional governments in the upper house, and significant power reserved to the regional level. The central government, however, has the ability to intervene in state or provincial affairs in some circumstances, particularly in the case of Argentina. Moreover, neither constitution assigns a formal role to the subnational governments in the process of amending the national constitution. In Argentina amendments must be passed by a nationally elected constitutional assembly. In Brazil amendments are passed by supermajorities of the two houses of the federal legislature but are not subject to ratification by the states. Mexico is a federal state, but both formally and informally it has long deviated from many principles of federalism. Formally, the upper house represents the states, but it is much weaker than the lower house. Informally, until the late 1980s a single highly centralized party controlled the federal government and all state governments, rendering subnational autonomy moot. With greater competition between parties, Mexico increasingly has come to resemble the federal state its constitution has long described.

The case of India is somewhat ambiguous. The Indian federal constitution spells out a long list of important subjects over which the states and territories that compose the union have exclusive jurisdiction. But the constitution gives the central government the power to legislate on any subject—including the ones reserved to the regional governments—it deems a matter of national importance. In addition, the central government has direct powers of control over the regional governments (e.g., the national Parliament can dissolve the legislative council of any state or territory).

The former Soviet Union was, by constitution, a federal state; but, apart from the nominal character of at least certain parts of its constitution, the constitutional role entrusted to the Communist Party unified the system to such an extent that the state was essentially unitary with some semifederal aspects. Post-Soviet Russia, in contrast, has a federal constitution in all respects.

Both Italy and Spain can be considered semifederal states, though Italy is much closer to the unitary model. The regions in these countries are endowed with legislative and administrative powers in certain areas, but all the courts are national. Italy is perhaps one of the best examples of how a state may closely resemble a unitary system notwithstanding the presence of regional governments. The limited powers constitutionally granted to the regions have been extended by the national legislature through its devolution of additional matters to the purview of regional legislatures. Regional laws, however, must respect general principles laid down in national statutes, and in practice little room is left for genuinely autonomous regional legislation. Moreover, the regions are not financially independent. Thus, on the whole they can be considered almost a branch of the system of local governments, on a par with communes and provinces, rather than a distinct third level of government.

UNITARY STATES

The United Kingdom often is cited as the quintessential example of a unitary state, despite the presence of regional governments. Northern Ireland has alternated between periods of special autonomy and direct rule by the British government; in the 1990s an autonomous government for the region was reestablished, though autonomy was sometimes suspended by the British government. Also in the 1990s a Scottish Parliament and a Welsh Assembly were established (the former, but not the latter, was given extensive powers, including taxation), and the government debated introducing assemblies in some English regions. In the absence of a rigid constitution at the national level, however, the powers of the regional parliaments remained ill-defined. Indeed, an act of the central

Parliament at Westminster theoretically could take powers away from the regional governments or in fact abolish them. Although France is a unitary state, in 1982 it established elective regional governments less dependent on the centre.

INTERNATIONAL UNIONS OF STATES

Beginning in the second half of the 20th century, there was a growing tendency in many countries to allow the direct operation within their constitutional systems of international laws and the laws of special international organizations to which they belonged. The constitutions of Germany and Italy, for example, require the legal system to conform with international customary law. Because both constitutions are rigid, this means that ordinary national statutes conflicting with such law are unconstitutional.

At various times, groups of nation-states have formed unions that resulted in the creation of supranational governmental agencies whose laws became part of the legal systems of the member states. Although these unions did not constitute a new political community in the strict sense, they did act as something like a new level of government above the ones already existing. The most important examples of such a system are the European Union (EU) and its predecessor organizations. The Treaty of Rome (1957), which established the European Community, created a government for the organization consisting of a commission, a council of ministers, an assembly (now the European Parliament), and a court (the European Court of Justice; ECJ). Directives and regulations enshrined in EU law must be applied by the national courts and must take precedence over national legislation. In addition, by adopting the euro, a single currency, member states agreed to cede substantial authority on financial management to the EU. The ECJ, which issues binding interpretations of the treaty and of EU regulations, allows for individual recourse.

In 2004 the heads of government of the EU signed a constitution that created the posts of president and foreign minister and expanded the powers of the European Parliament, though that constitution has since failed to be ratified. Under this constitution, the EU also was given a "legal personality," meaning that it could negotiate most treaties on behalf of its members. The EU may be the embryo of a future federal state, if the union develops into an organization whose central government is capable of making decisions independently of the consent of member states, and particularly if it is given substantial freedom to act in the field of foreign and military policy. Even as it exists now, however, the EU is much more than a simple alliance of states that issues regulations in its members' common economic interest. The structures of the EU penetrate deeply into the constitutional structures of the national member states, in much the same way as the structures of the central government penetrate those of regional governments in a federal system. Some features of federalism, such as the precedence of community law in member states and the restriction of interpretive functions to a central agency, are already present in the EU. Unlike state members of a true federal system, however, members of the EU may withdraw from the union at any time. But until a member takes such a step, it is subject to EU law in practically the same way that a subnational state or province is subject to federal law in a federal system.

EXECUTIVES AND LEGISLATURES

States may be classified as monarchical or republican and as having presidential or parliamentary executives. The

United States, which possesses a presidential government, and the United Kingdom, which is the oldest practitioner of parliamentary government, have long served as models of their respective systems of executive authority, both for scholarly analysis and for the drafting of the constitutions of other countries.

MONARCHICAL SYSTEMS

Although the institution of monarchy is as old as recorded history, since the beginning of the modern era many monarchies have been replaced with republics. Of the monarchies that remain—such as those in the United Kingdom, Japan, Spain, the Scandinavian countries, and the Low Countries (Belgium, the Netherlands, and Luxembourg)—many are best described as "constitutional monarchies": the monarchs are primarily titular heads of state and do not in fact possess important powers of government. Most of the executive powers are in the hands of ministers—headed by a prime minister—who are politically responsible to the parliament and not to the monarch. The executive powers of government in the United Kingdom, for example, are exercised by ministers who hold their offices by virtue of the fact that they command the support of a majority in the popularly elected House of Commons. A constitutional monarch can act only on the advice of the ministers. The position of the monarchs in Scandinavia and the Low Countries is similar to that of the monarch in Britain: they reign but do not rule. In countries where no political party has a majority of its own in the parliament, the monarch may exercise some discretion in deciding whom to invite to form a government. Even where they have this discretion, however, monarchs must first consult with the various party leaders, a requirement that severely limits their freedom of action. In countries with stable two-party systems, all the monarch can do is offer the prime ministership to the leader of the majority party. Since 1975 the Swedish king has not even possessed this formal power; it is the president of the legislative assembly who chooses and appoints the prime minister. A constitutional monarch is the head of the state, not of the government. Standing above the political controversies of the moment, the sovereign is an object of national pride and loyalty and a symbol of the nation's unity and its continuity with the past.

In a few monarchies, however—for example, those of Jordan, Morocco, and Saudi Arabia—the king exercises real powers of government. The ministers are chosen by and are responsible only to the king rather than to an elective parliamentary body. Hereditary rulers with this degree of personal power were quite common in the 18th century but are rare today. Although Jordan and Morocco have augmented the powers of their elected parliaments, the monarchs retain ultimate authority in those countries. In Thailand the constitution promulgated in 1932 greatly reduced the powers of the monarch, relegating him to a role similar to that of the European monarchs. Although he retained considerable formal powers, he could exercise them only upon the advice of elected leaders. His most important function was to serve as a living symbol of the country and as a focus of national unity.

PRESIDENTIAL SYSTEMS

By definition, presidential systems must possess three basic features. First, the president originates from outside the legislative authority. In most countries such presidents are elected directly by the citizens, though separation of origin can also be ensured through an electoral college (as in the United States or in Argentina before constitutional reforms were adopted in the mid-1990s), provided that legislators cannot also serve as electors. Second, the president serves simultaneously as head of government and head of state; he is empowered to select cabinet ministers, who are responsible to him and not to the legislative majority. And third, the president has some constitutionally guaranteed legislative authority.

The U.S. system is based on a strict concept of separation of powers: the executive, legislative, and judicial powers of government are vested by the Constitution in three separate branches. The president is neither selected by nor a member of the Congress. He is elected indirectly by the public through an electoral college for a fixed term of four years, and he holds office no matter how his legislative program fares in Congress and whether or not his political party controls either or both houses of Congress. (A president may be removed from office only for "Treason, Bribery, or other high Crimes and Misdemeanors"; removal requires impeachment by a majority of the House of Representatives followed by conviction by two-thirds of the Senate.) The members of the cabinet, as noted earlier, are chosen by the president and are politically responsible to him (though they must be confirmed by the Senate). The Constitution prohibits cabinet officials from serving simultaneously in Congress. Moreover, the president shares legislative powers with Congress: all bills passed by Congress are signed into law or vetoed by the president, though Congress may override a presidential veto by a two-thirds vote in each chamber.

Presidential systems may differ in important respects from the U.S. model. In terms of constitutional provisions, the most important variation is in the powers that the constitution delegates to the president. In contrast to the requirement of a supermajority in Congress to override a presidential veto in the United States, for example, in some countries (e.g., Brazil and Colombia), a presidential veto may be overridden by a simple majority. Many presidential constitutions (e.g., those in Argentina, Brazil, Colombia, and Russia) explicitly give the president the authority to introduce new laws by decree, thereby bypassing the legislature, though typically the legislature can rescind such laws after the fact.

Some countries with presidential systems require that cabinet appointments be approved by the legislature. Thus, in the United States the president's cabinet appointments must be confirmed by a majority vote of the Senate. In the Philippines appointments of cabinet ministers must be approved by a Commission on Appointments, which consists of members of both houses of the legislature. Once appointed, however, cabinet secretaries or ministers cannot be removed by the legislature, except by impeachment.

PARLIAMENTARY SYSTEMS

The executive is organized very differently in a parliamentary system. In the United Kingdom, whose Westminster system has been adopted in many countries, the executive branch is not entirely separate from the legislative branch. On the contrary, the British cabinet may be described as the leading committee of Parliament. Formerly, the British prime minister, the head of the government, could sit in either the House of Lords or the House of Commons, but contemporary convention dictates that he serve as a member of the House of Commons. The other ministers who make up the cabinet must be members of one or the other house of Parliament. If the prime minister wishes someone who is not in Parliament to serve in the cabinet, he must either appoint him to the peerage or find a vacancy in the House of Commons to which he can be elected.

Whereas the doctrine of separation of powers in the U.S. system does not require the executive branch to hold a majority in the legislature, in Great Britain the ministers of the crown hold office only so long as they enjoy the support of a majority in the House of Commons. A cabinet that loses such support must either dissolve the Commons and call a new election—thus in effect putting the issue to the voters—or resign and permit others to form a government. Since the start of the 20th century, most changes of government in Britain have occurred as a result of the outcome of a general election. It follows that in the British system the prime minister and the cabinet are fully in charge of Parliament. They are responsible, as the guiding committee of Parliament, for the preparation and enactment of most legislation and of the budget. There can be no permanent or serious conflict between the House of Commons and the cabinet, for responsibility means that the government of the day must either prevail or give way to another government. Thus, the deadlocks between the chief executive and the Congress that occur from time to time in the United States cannot occur in the British system.

Many parliamentary systems, however, lack the two-party system that typifies Britain's model of parliamentarism. Although there are in fact more than two parties in Britain, one party almost always holds a majority of seats, which thus enables the cabinet to be formed by ministers from a single party and prevents changes in the partisan complexion of the government between elections. Unless the government loses its majority before the next election (as a result of defections in the legislature or of by-elections to fill vacancies caused by death or resignation), the only event that can produce a change of government is an election that results in a legislative majority for another party.

In contrast, many other countries possess parliamentary systems in which it is rare for a single party to obtain a majority of seats. In such systems the cabinet may be formed by a coalition of two or more parties, or it may be formed by a party that lacks a majority in the parliament. Because a party may withdraw from a coalition over a policy or some other issue, and because the opposition may demonstrate through a vote of no confidence that the government has lost its majority, it is possible for the government to change between elections. In some of these countries, however, it is also possible for a government to persist in office despite a lack of majority support. In countries that have adopted a "constructive" vote of no confidence, for example, a government may be removed by the legislature between elections by a majority vote of no confidence only if a majority also elects a successor government. The constitution of the Federal Republic of Germany (1949–90) was the first to require a constructive vote of no confidence, its authors hoping to avoid the frequent votes of no confidence (without majority agreement on a replacement) that had typified executive-legislative relations during the Weimar Republic (1919–33). Constructive votes of no confidence also have been adopted in Hungary and Spain.

Parliamentary systems also vary in the role performed by the head of state. In constitutional monarchies the monarch occupies office by virtue of heredity. In parliamentary republics the head of state is usually a president. Presidents in parliamentary systems may be elected by direct popular vote (e.g., Ireland), by the legislature (e.g., the Czech Republic and Israel), or by an electoral college that consists of members of the legislature as well as delegates of regional assemblies (e.g., Germany, India, and Italy). They usually serve for fixed terms that are longer than the term of the parliament, and they may have some discretion in the appointment of a prime minister or the dissolution of the parliament.

OTHER SYSTEMS

Many constitutions with elected presidents do not meet the criteria of a presidential system outlined above. If the president must share—or, in some cases, cede—executive authority to a prime minister and cabinet depend on parliamentary confidence, then the system is neither presidential nor parliamentary but rather a hybrid. Such a system has been in place in France since the establishment of the Fifth Republic (1958). According to the terms of a constitutional amendment adopted in 1962, the president of the republic is elected by direct vote of the people for a seven-year term (shortened by referendum to five years in 2000). This mandate gives the president significant moral power because he is the only leader elected directly by the entire voting population. Although the exercise of some presidential powers requires the signature of the prime minister or of some other minister, the president is invested with broad powers of his own: he appoints the prime minister; he dominates the management of foreign relations; he may dissolve the National Assembly, though not more often than once a year; he may call a referendum; and he possesses vast emergency powers. In addition, he presides over the cabinet, known as the Council of Ministers. Members of the council cannot be members of the National Assembly or the Senate, but they have access to both chambers; they may speak there, though they do not vote. The cabinet is responsible to the National Assembly and can be dismissed by a motion of censure. Thus, the French system of government is not presidential because the president cannot maintain in office a cabinet that is opposed by a legislative majority. Although the president has the power to appoint the prime minister, he usually chooses the leader of the opposition party or coalition if it is in control of the National Assembly. Such periods of divided government are known in France as cohabitation.

Constitutions similar in key respects to that of France have been adopted in several countries, including Finland, Poland, Portugal, and Romania. Although the president's precise powers vary, in each of these countries he is popularly elected and has more than merely ceremonial powers, and the cabinet and prime minister are politically responsible to the legislature. In still other hybrid systems—including those of Peru, Russia, Sri Lanka, and Taiwan—the president retains more formal authority than the French president possesses during periods of cohabitation.

The Swiss executive is unique, having neither an elected presidency nor a cabinet responsible to the parliament. The executive is a Federal Council that consists of seven members elected for four-year terms by the legislature (the Federal Assembly). They are elected as individuals and are never forced to resign. Indeed, disagreement with the Federal Assembly leads neither to resignation of the Federal Council nor to dissolution of the parliament; the ministers simply adjust their positions to conform with the wishes of the parliamentary majority. This does not mean that the Federal Council is an unimportant body; as a group it originates most new legislation, and its members, as individuals, direct the major departments of government. Each year the legislature appoints a member of the Federal Council to serve as president of the confederation. The president is chairman of the Federal Council and titular head of state.

Although members of the Federal Council are formally elected as individuals, seats on the council have informally been apportioned according to a formula that gives each major party a certain number. From 1959 to 2003 the party composition of the Swiss executive remained the same, despite the shifting electoral strengths of the parties. Even after 2003 the Federal Council continued to consist of members of the four largest parties, which together regularly controlled more than four-fifths of the seats in the Federal Assembly.

UNICAMERAL AND BICAMERAL LEGISLATURES

A central feature of any constitution is the organization of the legislature. It may be a unicameral body with one chamber or a bicameral body with two chambers. Unicameral legislatures are typical in small countries with unitary systems of government (e.g., Denmark, Sweden, Finland, Israel, and New Zealand) or in very small countries (e.g., Andorra, Dominica, Luxembourg, Liechtenstein, Malta, and Tuvalu). Federal states, whether large or small, usually have bicameral legislatures, one house usually representing the main territorial subdivisions. The classic example is the Congress of the United States, which consists of a House of Representatives, with 435 members elected for two-year terms from single-member districts of approximately equal population, and a Senate, consisting of two persons from each state elected by the voters of that state. The fact that all states are represented equally in the Senate regardless of their size reflects the federal character of the American union. The U.S. Senate enjoys special powers not shared by the House of Representatives: it must ratify by a two-thirds majority vote the international treaties concluded by the president and must confirm the president's appointments to the cabinet and to other important executive offices. The federal character of the Swiss constitution is likewise reflected in the makeup of the country's national legislature, which is bicameral. One house, the National Council, consists of 200 members apportioned among the cantons according to population; the other house, the Council of States, consists of 46 members elected from the cantons by direct vote.

Argentina, Brazil, Mexico, and Russia possess federal systems that mirror the U.S. model of equal representation for each subnational government in the upper chamber (since the mid-1990s, one-fourth of Mexican senators have been elected in a single national district on the basis of the proportion of votes their political parties receive). In some federal systems representation of regions in the upper house is not equal. In Germany, for example, states are allocated three to six seats in the upper house (the Bundesrat), depending on population. In federal Austria each state is guaranteed at least three seats in the Bundesrat. In federations in which there is no guaranteed overrepresentation of smaller regions, a crucial principle of federalism is violated: the protection of regional sovereignty against a central government, backed by a national majority, that may seek to erode regional autonomy. An example of this case is Canada, where the upper house (the Senate) is an appointed body that is not constitutionally required to represent the provinces, though in practice senators are appointed (for life terms) to ensure regional balance. Although Micronesia and Venezuela are both federal states, each has a unicameral legislature.

A unitary system of government does not necessarily imply unicameralism. In fact, the legislatures of most countries with unitary systems are bicameral, though one chamber is usually more powerful than the other. The United Kingdom, for example, has a unitary system with a bicameral legislature, which consists of the House of Lords and the House of Commons. The Commons has become by far the more powerful of the two chambers, and the cabinet is politically responsible only to it. The

Lords has no control over finances and only a modest suspensory veto with respect to other legislation (it may delay the implementation of legislation but not kill it). A veto by the Lords can be overcome in the Commons by a second vote at an early date. The parliaments of Italy, Japan, and France also are bicameral, though none of those countries has a federal form of government. Although in the United States all 50 states except Nebraska have bicameral legislatures, their governmental systems are unitary. In the 49 U.S. states with bicameral legislatures, the two houses have equal legislative authority, but the so-called upper houses—usually called senates—have the special function of confirming the governors' appointments.

JUDICIAL REVIEW

The first examples of written constitutions came from the United States. The United States also gave the world an institution that has become a fundamental feature of many contemporary constitutional systems: judicial review, or the power of the courts of a country to examine the actions of the legislative, executive, and administrative arms of the government and to determine whether such actions are consistent with the constitution. Actions judged inconsistent are declared unconstitutional and, therefore, null and void. The institution of judicial review in this sense depends upon the existence of a written constitution. The conventional usage of the term judicial review could be more accurately described as "constitutional review" because there also exists a long practice of judicial review of the actions of administrative agencies that require neither that courts have the power to declare those actions unconstitutional nor that the country have a written constitution. Such "administrative review" assesses the allegedly questionable actions of administrators against standards of reasonableness and abuse of discretion. When courts determine that challenged administration actions are unreasonable or involve abuses of discretion, those actions are declared null and void, as are actions that are judged inconsistent with constitutional requirements when courts exercise judicial review in the conventional or constitutional sense. Whether or not a court has the power to declare the acts of government agencies unconstitutional, it can achieve the same effect by exercising "indirect" judicial review. In such cases the court pronounces that a challenged rule or action could not have been intended by the legislature because it is inconsistent with some other laws or established legal principles. Constitutional judicial review is usually considered to have begun with the assertion by John Marshall, chief justice of the United States (1801–35), in *Marbury* v. *Madison* (1803), that the Supreme Court of the United States had the power to invalidate legislation enacted by Congress. There was, however, no express warrant for Marshall's assertion of the power of judicial review in the actual text of the Constitution of the United States; its success rested ultimately on the Supreme Court's own ruling, plus the absence of effective political challenge to it.

Constitutional judicial review exists in several forms. In countries that follow U.S. practice (e.g., Kenya and New Zealand), judicial review can be exercised only in concrete cases or controversies and only after the fact—i.e., only laws that are in effect or actions that have already occurred can be found to be unconstitutional, and then only when they involve a specific dispute between litigants. In France judicial review must take place in the abstract (i.e., in the absence of an actual case or controversy) and before promulgation (i.e., before a challenged law has taken effect). In other countries (e.g., Austria, Germany, South Korea, and Spain) courts can exercise judicial review only after a law has taken effect, though they can do so either in the

Supreme Court Justice John Marshall believed that the United States should develop a strong federal government; he therefore interpreted the Constitution in such a way as to expand the role of the Court. In his ruling in Marbury v. Madison, *Marshall declared that the Court had the power to invalidate any act of Congress—and hence of a state legislature—that it thought contrary to the federal Constitution.* Stock Montage/Archive Photos/Getty Images

abstract or in concrete cases. Systems of constitutional judicial review also differ in the extent to which they allow courts to exercise it. For example, in the United States all courts have the power to entertain claims of unconstitutionality, but in some countries (e.g., France, Germany, New Zealand, and South Africa) only specialized constitutional courts can hear such claims.

A number of the constitutions drafted in Europe and Asia after World War II incorporated judicial review in various forms. For example, in France, where the Cour de Cassation (the highest court of criminal and civil appeal) has no power of judicial review, a constitutional council (Conseil Constitutionnel) of mixed judicial-legislative character was established; Germany, Italy, and South Korea created special constitutional courts; and India, Japan, and Pakistan set up supreme courts to exercise judicial review in the manner generally used in the United States and in the British Commonwealth.

After World War II many countries felt strong pressure to adopt judicial review, a result of the influence of U.S. constitutional ideas—particularly the idea that a system of constitutional checks and balances is an essential element of democratic government. Some observers concluded that the concentration of government power in the executive, substantially unchecked by other agencies of government, contributed to the rise of totalitarian regimes in Germany and Japan in the era between World War I and World War II. Although judicial review had been relatively uncommon before World War II, by the early 21st century more than 100 countries had specifically incorporated judicial review into their constitutions. (This number does not include the United States, whose constitution still includes no mention of the practice.)

CONCLUSION

As discussed in Chapter 4, one general way of classifying constitutions is by whether or not the procedure used to modify them is substantially different from that used to enact ordinary laws. Constitutions that stipulate distinct rules for changes to themselves are called "rigid"; those that do not are called "flexible." Similar terminology has been used in the analysis of general characteristics that tend to make constitutions successful or unsuccessful. The most successful constitutional systems tend to combine procedural stability with substantive flexibility—that is, they preserve the same general rules of political procedure from one generation to the next while at the same time facilitating adaptation to changing circumstances. By reference to such criteria, those written constitutions that have achieved the greatest success—the U.S. Constitution being a prime example—are comparatively short; confine themselves in the main to matters of procedure (including their own amendment) rather than matters of substance; keep their substantive provisions (to the extent that they contain them at all) rather vague and generalized; and contain procedures that are congruent with popular political experience and know-how. These general characteristics appear to be more important to the success of a constitution than such particular arrangements as the relations between various organs and levels of government or the powers, functions, and terms of tenure of different officers of state.

As also discussed in Chapter 4, of particular importance to the success of constitutions are political values and attitudes and the extent to which they are congruent with the formal prescriptions and proscriptions of the constitution itself. Constitutional government cannot survive effectively in situations in which the constitution prescribes a set of values or manner of conducting affairs that is alien to the customs and way of thinking of the people. When, as happened in many developing countries in the decades after World War II, a new and alien kind of constitutional democracy is imposed or adopted, a gap may soon develop between constitutionally prescribed and actual governmental practice. This in turn renders the government susceptible to attack by opposition groups. Such attack is especially easy to mount in situations in which a constitution has a heavy and detailed substantive content—when, for example, it guarantees the right to gainful employment or the right to a university education for all qualified candidates. In the event of the government being unable to fulfill its commitment, the opposition is able to call the constitution a mere scrap of paper and to demand its improvement or even its complete replacement. Such tactics often have succeeded, but they ignore the dual strategic function of constitutions: they are meant not only to arrange the offices of the government but also to state the goals toward which the authors and ratifiers of the constitution want their community to move.

Through its deft combination of procedural stability and substantive flexibility, as well as through the compatibility of the framers' vision with the broader political values and attitudes of the American population, the U.S. Constitution has proved itself a dynamic, living document and one of the most successful constitutions in history. It has served as a model for other countries, its provisions being widely imitated in national constitutions throughout the world. Although its brevity and ambiguity have sometimes led to serious disputes about its meaning, they also have made it adaptable to changing historical circumstances and ensured its relevance in ages far removed from the one in which it was written.

Constitution of the United States (1787)

We the People of the United States, in Order to form a more perfect Union, establish Justice, insure domestic Tranquility, provide for the common defence, promote the general Welfare, and secure the Blessings of Liberty to ourselves and our Posterity, do ordain and establish this Constitution for the United States of America.

ARTICLE I

Section 1—All legislative Powers herein granted shall be vested in a Congress of the United States, which shall consist of a Senate and House of Representatives.

Section 2—1 The House of Representatives shall be composed of Members chosen every second Year by the People of the several States, and the Electors in each State shall have the Qualifications requisite for Electors of the most numerous Branch of the State Legislature.

2 No person shall be a Representative who shall not have attained to the Age of twenty five Years, and been seven Years a Citizen of the United States, and who shall not, when elected, be an Inhabitant of that State in which he shall be chosen.

3 [Representatives and direct Taxes shall be apportioned among the several States which may be

included within this Union, according to their respective Numbers, which shall be determined by adding to the whole Number of free Persons, including those bound to Service for a Term of Years, and excluding Indians not taxed, three fifths of all other Persons.]{2} The actual Enumeration shall be made within three Years after the first Meeting of the Congress of the United States, and within every subsequent Term of ten Years, in such Manner as they shall by Law direct. The Number of Representatives shall not exceed one for every thirty Thousand, but each State shall have at Least one Representative; and until such enumeration shall be made, the State of New Hampshire shall be entitled to chuse three, Massachusetts eight, Rhode-Island and Providence Plantations one, Connecticut five, New-York six, New Jersey four, Pennsylvania eight, Delaware one, Maryland six, Virginia ten, North Carolina five, South Carolina five, and Georgia three.

4 When vacancies happen in the Representation from any State, the Executive Authority thereof shall issue Writs of Election to fill such Vacancies.

5 The House of Representatives shall chuse their Speaker and other Officers; and shall have the sole Power of Impeachment.

Section 3—1 The Senate of the United States shall be composed of two Senators from each State, [chosen by the Legislature thereof,]{3} for six Years; and each Senator shall have one Vote.

2 Immediately after they shall be assembled in Consequence of the first Election, they shall be divided as equally as may be into three Classes. The Seats of the Senators of the first Class shall be vacated at the Expiration of the second Year, of the second Class at the Expiration of the fourth Year, and of the third Class at the Expiration of the sixth Year, so that one third

may be chosen every second Year; [and if Vacancies happen by Resignation, or otherwise, during the Recess of the Legislature of any State, the Executive thereof may make temporary Appointments until the next Meeting of the Legislature, which shall then fill such Vacancies].{4}3 No Person shall be a Senator who shall not have attained to the Age of thirty Years, and been nine Years a Citizen of the United States, and who shall not, when elected, be an Inhabitant of that State for which he shall be chosen.

4 The Vice President of the United States shall be President of the Senate, but shall have no Vote, unless they be equally divided.

5 The Senate shall chuse their other Officers, and also a President pro tempore, in the Absence of the Vice President, or when he shall exercise the Office of President of the United States.

6 The Senate shall have the sole Power to try all Impeachments. When sitting for that Purpose, they shall be on Oath or Affirmation. When the President of the United States is tried, the Chief Justice shall preside: And no Person shall be convicted without the Concurrence of two thirds of the Members present.

7 Judgment in Cases of Impeachment shall not extend further than to removal from Office, and disqualification to hold and enjoy any Office of honor, Trust or Profit under the United States: but the Party convicted shall nevertheless be liable and subject to Indictment, Trial, Judgment and Punishment, according to Law.

Section 4—1 The Times, Places and Manner of holding Elections for Senators and Representatives, shall be prescribed in each State by the Legislature thereof; but the Congress may at any time by Law make or alter such Regulations, except as to the Places of chusing Senators.

2 The Congress shall assemble at least once in every Year, and such Meeting shall [be on the first Monday in December,]{5} unless they shall by Law appoint a different Day.

Section 5—1 Each House shall be the Judge of the Elections, Returns and Qualifications of its own Members, and a Majority of each shall constitute a Quorum to do Business; but a smaller Number may adjourn from day to day, and may be authorized to compel the Attendance of absent Members, in such Manner, and under such Penalties as each House may provide.

2 Each House may determine the Rules of its Proceedings, punish its Members for disorderly Behaviour, and, with the Concurrence of two thirds, expel a Member.

3 Each House shall keep a Journal of its Proceedings, and from time to time publish the same, excepting such Parts as may in their Judgment require Secrecy; and the Yeas and Nays of the Members of either House on any question shall, at the Desire of one fifth of those Present, be entered on the Journal.

4 Neither House, during the Session of Congress, shall, without the Consent of the other, adjourn for more than three days, nor to any other Place than that in which the two Houses shall be sitting.

Section 6—1 The Senators and Representatives shall receive a Compensation for their Services, to be ascertained by Law, and paid out of the Treasury of the United States. They shall in all Cases, except Treason, Felony and Breach of the Peace, be privileged from Arrest during their Attendance at the Session of their respective Houses, and in going to and returning from the same; and for any Speech or Debate in either House, they shall not be questioned in any other Place.

2 No Senator or Representative shall, during the Time

for which he was elected, be appointed to any civil Office under the Authority of the United States, which shall have been created, or the Emoluments whereof shall have been encreased during such time; and no Person holding any Office under the United States, shall be a Member of either House during his Continuance in Office.

Section 7—1 All Bills for raising Revenue shall originate in the House of Representatives; but the Senate may propose or concur with Amendments as on other Bills.

2 Every Bill which shall have passed the House of Representatives and the Senate, shall, before it become a Law, be presented to the President of the United States; If he approve he shall sign it, but if not he shall return it, with his Objections to that House in which it shall have originated, who shall enter the Objections at large on their Journal, and proceed to reconsider it. If after such Reconsideration two thirds of that House shall agree to pass the Bill, it shall be sent, together with the Objections, to the other House, by which it shall likewise be reconsidered, and if approved by two thirds of that House, it shall become a Law. But in all such Cases the Votes of both Houses shall be determined by yeas and Nays, and the Names of the Persons voting for and against the Bill shall be entered on the Journal of each House respectively. If any Bill shall not be returned by the President within ten Days (Sundays excepted) after it shall have been presented to him, the Same shall be a Law, in like Manner as if he had signed it, unless the Congress by their Adjournment prevent its Return, in which Case it shall not be a Law.

3 Every Order, Resolution, or Vote to which the Concurrence of the Senate and House of Representatives may be necessary (except on a question of Adjournment) shall be presented to the

President of the United States; and before the Same shall take Effect, shall be approved by him, or being disapproved by him, shall be repassed by two thirds of the Senate and House of Representatives, according to the Rules and Limitations prescribed in the Case of a Bill.

Section 8—1 The Congress shall have Power To lay and collect Taxes, Duties, Imposts and Excises, to pay the Debts and provide for the common Defence and general Welfare of the United States; but all Duties, Imposts and Excises shall be uniform throughout the United States;

2 To borrow Money on the credit of the United States;

3 To regulate Commerce with foreign Nations, and among the several States, and with the Indian Tribes;

4 To establish an uniform Rule of Naturalization, and uniform Laws on the subject of Bankruptcies throughout the United States;

5 To coin Money, regulate the Value thereof, and of foreign Coin, and fix the Standard of Weights and Measures;

6 To provide for the Punishment of counterfeiting the Securities and current Coin of the United States;

7 To establish Post Offices and post Roads;

8 To promote the Progress of Science and useful Arts, by securing for limited Times to Authors and Inventors the exclusive Right to their respective Writings and Discoveries;

9 To constitute Tribunals inferior to the supreme Court;

10 To define and punish Piracies and Felonies committed on the high Seas, and Offences against the Law of Nations;

11 To declare War, grant Letters of Marque and Reprisal, and make Rules concerning Captures on

Land and Water;

12 To raise and support Armies, but no Appropriation of Money to that Use shall be for a longer Term than two Years;

13 To provide and maintain a Navy;

14 To make Rules for the Government and Regulation of the land and naval Forces;

15 To provide for calling forth the Militia to execute the Laws of the Union, suppress Insurrections and repel Invasions;

16 To provide for organizing, arming, and disciplining, the Militia, and for governing such Part of them as may be employed in the Service of the United States, reserving to the States respectively, the Appointment of the Officers, and the Authority of training the Militia according to the discipline prescribed by Congress;

17 To exercise exclusive Legislation in all Cases whatsoever, over such District (not exceeding ten Miles square) as may, by Cession of particular States, and the Acceptance of Congress, become the Seat of the Government of the United States, and to exercise like Authority over all Places purchased by the Consent of the Legislature of the State in which the Same shall be, for the Erection of Forts, Magazines, Arsenals, dock-Yards, and other needful Buildings;—And

18 To make all Laws which shall be necessary and proper for carrying into Execution the foregoing Powers, and all other Powers vested by this Constitution in the Government of the United States, or in any Department or Officer thereof.

Section 9—1 The Migration or Importation of such Persons as any of the States now existing shall think proper to admit, shall not be prohibited by the Congress prior to the Year one thousand eight hundred and eight, but a Tax or duty may be imposed on such Importation, not exceeding ten dollars for each Person.

2 The Privilege of the Writ of Habeas Corpus shall not be suspended, unless when in Cases of Rebellion or Invasion the public Safety may require it.

3 No Bill of Attainder or ex post facto Law shall be passed.

4 No Capitation, or other direct, Tax shall be laid, unless in Proportion to the Census or Enumeration herein before directed to be taken.{6}

5 No Tax or Duty shall be laid on Articles exported from any State.

6 No Preference shall be given by any Regulation of Commerce or Revenue to the Ports of one State over those of another: nor shall Vessels bound to, or from, one State, be obliged to enter, clear, or pay Duties in another.

7 No Money shall be drawn from the Treasury, but in Consequence of Appropriations made by Law; and a regular Statement and Account of the Receipts and Expenditures of all public Money shall be published from time to time.

8 No Title of Nobility shall be granted by the United States: And no Person holding any Office of Profit or Trust under them, shall, without the Consent of the Congress, accept of any present, Emolument, Office, or Title, of any kind whatever, from any King, Prince, or foreign State.

Section 10—1 No State shall enter into any Treaty, Alliance, or Confederation; grant Letters of Marque and Reprisal; coin Money; emit Bills of Credit; make any Thing but gold and silver Coin a Tender in Payment of Debts; pass any Bill of Attainder, ex post facto Law, or Law impairing the Obligation of Contracts, or grant any Title of Nobility.

2 No State shall, without the Consent of the Congress,

lay any Imposts or Duties on Imports or Exports, except what may be absolutely necessary for executing it's inspection Laws: and the net Produce of all Duties and Imposts, laid by any State on Imports or Exports, shall be for the Use of the Treasury of the United States; and all such Laws shall be subject to the Revision and Controul of the Congress.

3 No State shall, without the Consent of Congress, lay any Duty of Tonnage, keep Troops, or Ships of War in time of Peace, enter into any Agreement or Compact with another State, or with a foreign Power, or engage in War, unless actually invaded, or in such imminent Danger as will not admit of delay.

ARTICLE II

Section I—1 The executive Power shall be vested in a President of the United States of America. He shall hold his Office during the Term of four Years, and, together with the Vice President, chosen for the same Term, be elected, as follows

2 Each State shall appoint, in such Manner as the Legislature thereof may direct, a Number of Electors, equal to the whole Number of Senators and Representatives to which the State may be entitled in the Congress: but no Senator or Representative, or Person holding an Office of Trust or Profit under the United States, shall be appointed an Elector.[The Electors shall meet in their respective States, and vote by Ballot for two Persons, of whom one at least shall not be an Inhabitant of the same State with themselves. And they shall make a List of all the Persons voted for, and of the Number of Votes for each; which List they shall sign and certify, and transmit sealed to the Seat of the Government of the United States, directed

to the President of the Senate. The President of the Senate shall, in the Presence of the Senate and House of Representatives, open all the Certificates, and the Votes shall then be counted. The Person having the greatest Number of Votes shall be the President, if such Number be a Majority of the whole Number of Electors appointed; and if there be more than one who have such Majority, and have an equal Number of Votes, then the House of Representatives shall immediately chuse by Ballot one of them for President; and if no Person have a Majority, then from the five highest on the List the said House shall in like Manner chuse the President. But in chusing the President, the Votes shall be taken by States, the Representation from each State having one Vote; A quorum for this Purpose shall consist of a Member or Members from two thirds of the States, and a Majority of all the States shall be necessary to a Choice. In every Case, after the Choice of the President, the Person having the greatest Number of Votes of the Electors shall be the Vice President. But if there should remain two or more who have equal Votes, the Senate shall chuse from them by Ballot the Vice President.]{7}

3 The Congress may determine the Time of chusing the Electors, and the Day on which they shall give their Votes; which Day shall be the same throughout the United States.

4 No Person except a natural born Citizen, or a Citizen of the United States, at the time of the Adoption of this Constitution, shall be eligible to the Office of President; neither shall any Person be eligible to that Office who shall not have attained to the Age of thirty five Years, and been fourteen Years a Resident within the United States.

5 In Case of the Removal of the President from Office, or of his Death, Resignation, or Inability to discharge

the Powers and Duties of the said Office,{8} the Same shall devolve on the Vice President, and the Congress may by Law provide for the Case of Removal, Death, Resignation or Inability, both of the President and Vice President, declaring what Officer shall then act as President, and such Officer shall act accordingly, until the Disability be removed, or a President shall be elected.

6 The President shall, at stated Times, receive for his Services, a Compensation, which shall neither be encreased nor diminished during the Period for which he shall have been elected, and he shall not receive within that Period any other Emolument from the United States, or any of them.

7 Before he enter on the Execution of his Office, he shall take the following Oath or Affirmation:—"I do solemnly swear (or affirm) that I will faithfully execute the Office of President of the United States, and will to the best of my Ability, preserve, protect and defend the Constitution of the United States."

Section 2—1 The President shall be Commander in Chief of the Army and Navy of the United States, and of the Militia of the several States, when called into the actual Service of the United States; he may require the Opinion, in writing, of the principal Officer in each of the executive Departments, upon any Subject relating to the Duties of their respective Offices, and he shall have Power to grant Reprieves and Pardons for Offences against the United States, except in Cases of Impeachment.

2 He shall have Power, by and with the Advice and Consent of the Senate, to make Treaties, provided two thirds of the Senators present concur; and he shall nominate, and by and with the Advice and Consent of the Senate, shall appoint Ambassadors,

other public Ministers and Consuls, Judges of the supreme Court, and all other Officers of the United States, whose Appointments are not herein otherwise provided for, and which shall be established by Law: but the Congress may by Law vest the Appointment of such inferior Officers, as they think proper, in the President alone, in the Courts of Law, or in the Heads of Departments.

3 The President shall have Power to fill up all Vacancies that may happen during the Recess of the Senate, by granting Commissions which shall expire at the End of their next Session.

Section 3—He shall from time to time give to the Congress Information of the State of the Union, and recommend to their Consideration such Measures as he shall judge necessary and expedient; he may, on extraordinary Occasions, convene both Houses, or either of them, and in Case of Disagreement between them, with Respect to the Time of Adjournment, he may adjourn them to such Time as he shall think proper; he shall receive Ambassadors and other public Ministers; he shall take Care that the Laws be faithfully executed, and shall Commission all the Officers of the United States.

Section 4—The President, Vice President and all civil Officers of the United States, shall be removed from Office on Impeachment for, and Conviction of, Treason, Bribery, or other high Crimes and Misdemeanors.

ARTICLE III

Section 1—The judicial Power of the United States, shall be vested in one supreme Court, and in such inferior Courts as the Congress may from time to time ordain and establish. The Judges, both of the supreme and inferior Courts, shall hold their Offices during good Behaviour, and shall, at stated Times, receive for their Services, a Compensation, which shall not be diminished during their Continuance in Office.

Section 2—1 The judicial Power shall extend to all Cases, in Law and Equity, arising under this Constitution, the Laws of the United States, and Treaties made, or which shall be made, under their Authority;—to all Cases affecting Ambassadors, other public Ministers and Consuls;—to all Cases of admiralty and maritime Jurisdiction;—to Controversies to which the United States shall be a Party;—to Controversies between two or more States;—between a State and Citizens of another State;{9}—between Citizens of different States,—between Citizens of the same State claiming Lands under Grants of different States, and between a State, or the Citizens thereof, and foreign States, Citizens or Subjects.

2 In all Cases affecting Ambassadors, other public Ministers and Consuls, and those in which a State shall be Party, the supreme Court shall have original Jurisdiction. In all the other Cases before mentioned, the supreme Court shall have appellate Jurisdiction, both as to Law and Fact, with such Exceptions, and under such Regulations as the Congress shall make.

3 The Trial of all Crimes, except in Cases of Impeachment, shall be by Jury; and such Trial shall be held in the State where the said Crimes shall have been committed; but when not committed within any State, the Trial shall be at such Place or Places as the Congress may by Law have directed.

Section 3—1 Treason against the United States, shall consist only in levying War against them, or in adhering to their Enemies, giving them Aid and Comfort. No

Person shall be convicted of Treason unless on the Testimony of two Witnesses to the same overt Act, or on Confession in open Court.

2 The Congress shall have Power to declare the Punishment of Treason, but no Attainder of Treason shall work Corruption of Blood, or Forfeiture except during the Life of the Person attainted.

ARTICLE IV

Section 1—Full Faith and Credit shall be given in each State to the public Acts, Records, and judicial Proceedings of every other State. And the Congress may by general Laws prescribe the Manner in which such Acts, Records and Proceedings shall be proved, and the Effect thereof.

Section 2—1 The Citizens of each State shall be entitled to all Privileges and Immunities of Citizens in the several States.

2 A Person charged in any State with Treason, Felony, or other Crime, who shall flee from Justice, and be found in another State, shall on Demand of the executive Authority of the State from which he fled, be delivered up, to be removed to the State having Jurisdiction of the Crime.

3 [No Person held to Service or Labour in one State, under the Laws thereof, escaping into another, shall, in Consequence of any Law or Regulation therein, be discharged from such Service or Labour, but shall be delivered up on Claim of the Party to whom such Service or Labour may be due.]{10}

Section 3—1 New States may be admitted by the Congress into this Union; but no new State shall be formed or erected within the Jurisdiction of any other State; nor any State be formed by the Junction of two or more States, or Parts of States, without the Consent of the Legislatures of the States concerned as well as of the Congress.

2 The Congress shall have Power to dispose of and make all needful Rules and Regulations respecting the Territory or other Property belonging to the United States; and nothing in this Constitution shall be so construed as to Prejudice any Claims of the United States, or of any particular State.

Section 4—The United States shall guarantee to every State in this Union a Republican Form of Government, and shall protect each of them against Invasion; and on Application of the Legislature, or of the Executive (when the Legislature cannot be convened) against domestic Violence.

ARTICLE V

The Congress, whenever two thirds of both Houses shall deem it necessary, shall propose Amendments to this Constitution, or, on the Application of the Legislatures of two thirds of the several States, shall call a Convention for proposing Amendments, which, in either Case, shall be valid to all Intents and Purposes, as Part of this Constitution, when ratified by the Legislatures of three fourths of the several States, or by Conventions in three fourths thereof, as the one or the other Mode of Ratification may be proposed by the Congress; Provided [that no Amendment which may be made prior to the Year One thousand eight hundred and eight shall in any Manner affect the first and fourth Clauses in the Ninth Section of the first Article; and]{11} that no State, without its Consent, shall be deprived of its equal Suffrage in the Senate.

ARTICLE VI

1 All Debts contracted and Engagements entered into, before the Adoption of this Constitution, shall be as valid against the United States under this Constitution, as under the Confederation.
2 This Constitution, and the Laws of the United States which shall be made in Pursuance thereof; and all Treaties made, or which shall be made, under the Authority of the United States, shall be the supreme Law of the Land; and the Judges in every State shall be bound thereby, any Thing in the Constitution or Laws of any State to the Contrary notwithstanding.
3 The Senators and Representatives before mentioned, and the Members of the several State Legislatures, and all executive and judicial Officers, both of the United States and of the several States, shall be bound by Oath or Affirmation, to support this Constitution; but no religious Test shall ever be required as a Qualification to any Office or public Trust under the United States.

ARTICLE VII

The Ratification of the Conventions of nine States, shall be sufficient for the Establishment of this Constitution between the States so ratifying the Same.

Done in Convention by the Unanimous Consent of the States present the Seventeenth Day of September in the Year of our Lord one thousand seven hundred and Eighty seven and of the Independence of the United States of America the Twelfth
IN WITNESS whereof We have hereunto subscribed our Names,
Go. WASHINGTON
Presidt. and deputy from Virginia

New Hampshire
John Langdon
Nicholas Gilman
Massachusetts
Nathaniel Gorham
Rufus King
Connecticut
Wm. Saml. Johnson
Roger Sherman
New York
Alexander Hamilton
New Jersey
Wil: Livingston
David Brearley
Wm. Paterson
Jona: Dayton
Pennsylvania
B Franklin
Thomas Mifflin
Robt Morris
Geo. Clymer
Thos. FitzSimons
Jared Ingersoll
James Wilson
Gouv Morris
Delaware
Geo: Read
Gunning Bedford jun
John Dickinson
Richard Bassett
Jaco: Broom
Maryland
James McHenry
Dan of St Thos. Jenifer
Danl Carroll

*Virginia*John Blair—
James Madison Jr.
North Carolina
Wm. Blount
Rich'd Dobbs Spaight
Hu Williamson
South Carolina
. Rutledge
Charles Cotesworth Pinckney
Charles Pinckney
Pierce Butler
*Georgia*William Few
Abr BaldwinAttest:
William Jackson, *Secretary*

AMENDMENTS

Articles in addition to, and amendment of, The Constitution of the United States of America, proposed by Congress, and ratified by the legislatures of the several states pursuant to the fifth article of the original Constitution.

The first 10 amendments to the Constitution were proposed by the Congress on Sept. 25, 1789. They were ratified by the following states, and the notifications of the ratification by the governors thereof were successively communicated by the President to the Congress: New Jersey, Nov. 20, 1789; Maryland, Dec. 19, 1789; North Carolina, Dec. 22, 1789; South Carolina, Jan. 19, 1790; New Hampshire, Jan. 25, 1790; Delaware, Jan. 28, 1790; New York, Feb. 4, 1790; Pennsylvania, March 10, 1790; Rhode Island, June 7, 1790; Vermont, Nov. 3, 1791; and Virginia, Dec. 15, 1791. Ratification was completed on Dec. 15, 1791.

The amendments were subsequently ratified by Massachusetts, March 2, 1939; Georgia, March 18, 1939; and Connecticut, April 19, 1939.

Two other amendments were concurrently proposed in 1789. One failed of ratification. The other (Amendment XXVII) was not ratified until May 7, 1992, when the Michigan legislature gave it the required number of state approvals.

Amendment [I]{12} Congress shall make no law respecting an establishment of religion, or prohibiting the free exercise thereof; or abridging the freedom of speech, or of the press; or the right of the people peaceably to assemble, and to petition the Government for a redress of grievances.

Amendment [II] A well regulated Militia, being necessary to the security of a free State, the right of the people to keep and bear Arms, shall not be infringed.

Amendment [III] No Soldier shall, in time of peace be quartered in any house, without the consent of the Owner, nor in time of war, but in a manner to be prescribed by law.

Amendment [IV] The right of the people to be secure in their persons, houses, papers, and effects, against unreasonable searches and seizures, shall not be violated, and no Warrants shall issue, but upon probable cause, supported by Oath or affirmation, and particularly describing the place to be searched, and the persons or things to be seized.

Amendment [V] No person shall be held to answer for a capital, or otherwise infamous crime, unless on a presentment or indictment of a Grand Jury, except in cases arising in the land or naval forces, or in the Militia, when in actual service in time of War or public danger; nor shall any person be subject for the same offence to be twice put in jeopardy of life or limb; nor shall be compelled in any criminal case to be a witness against himself, nor be deprived of life, liberty, or property, without due process of law; nor shall private property be taken for public use without just compensation.

Amendment [VI] In all criminal prosecutions, the accused shall enjoy the right to a speedy and public trial, by an impartial jury of the State and district wherein the crime shall have been committed, which district shall have been previously ascertained by law, and to be informed of the nature and cause of the accusation; to be confronted with the witnesses against him; to have compulsory process for obtaining Witnesses in his favor, and to have the assistance of counsel for his defence.

Amendment [VII] In Suits at common law, where the value in controversy shall exceed twenty dollars, the right of trial by jury shall be preserved, and no fact tried by a jury, shall be otherwise reexamined in any Court of the United States, than according to the rules of the common law.

Amendment [VIII] Excessive bail shall not be required, nor excessive fines imposed, nor cruel and unusual punishments inflicted.

Amendment [IX] The enumeration in the Constitution, of certain rights, shall not be construed to deny or disparage others retained by the people. Amendment [X] The powers not delegated to the United States by the Constitution, nor prohibited by it to the States, are reserved to the States respectively, or to the people.

Amendment [XI] [1795] The Judicial power of the United States shall not be construed to extend to any suit in law or equity, commenced or prosecuted against one of the United States by Citizens of another State, or by Citizens or Subjects of any Foreign State.

Amendment [XII] [1804] The electors shall meet in their respective states and vote by ballot for President and Vice President, one of whom, at least, shall not be an inhabitant of the same state with themselves; they shall name in their ballots the person voted for as President, and in distinct ballots the person voted for as Vice President, and they shall make distinct lists of all persons voted for as President, and of all persons voted for as Vice President, and of the number of votes for each, which lists they shall sign and certify, and transmit sealed to the seat of the government of the United States, directed to the President of the Senate;—The President of the Senate shall, in the presence of the Senate and House of Representatives, open all the certificates and the votes shall then be counted;—The person having the greatest number of votes for President, shall be the President, if such number be a majority of the whole number of Electors appointed; and if no person have such majority, then from the persons having the highest numbers not exceeding three on the list of those voted for as President, the House of Representatives shall choose immediately, by ballot, the President. But in choosing the President, the votes shall be taken by states, the representation from each state having one vote; a quorum for this purpose shall consist of a member or members from two-thirds of the states, and a majority of all the states shall be necessary to a choice. [And if the House of Representatives shall not choose a President whenever the right of choice shall devolve upon them, before the fourth day of March next following, then the Vice President shall act as President, as in the case of the death or other constitutional disability of the President.]{13} The person having the greatest number of votes as Vice President, shall be the Vice President, if such number be a majority of the whole number of Electors appointed, and if no person have a majority, then from the two highest numbers on the list, the Senate shall choose the Vice President; a quorum for the purpose shall consist of two-thirds of the whole number of Senators, and a majority of the whole number shall be necessary to a choice. But no person constitutionally ineligible to the office of President shall be eligible to that of Vice President of the United States.

Amendment XIII [1865] *Section 1*—Neither slavery nor involuntary servitude, except as a punishment for crime whereof the party shall have been duly convicted, shall exist within the United States, or any place subject to their jurisdiction.

Section 2—Congress shall have power to enforce this article by appropriate legislation.

Amendment XIV [1868] *Section 1*—All persons born or naturalized in the United States, and subject to the jurisdiction thereof, are citizens of the United States and of the State wherein they reside. No State shall make or enforce any law which shall abridge the privileges or immunities of citizens of the United States; nor shall any State deprive any person of life, liberty, or property, without due process of law; nor deny to any person within its jurisdiction the equal protection of the laws.

Section 2—Representatives shall be apportioned among the several States according to their respective numbers, counting the whole number of persons in each State, excluding Indians not taxed. But when the right to vote at any election for the choice of electors for President and Vice President of the United States, Representatives in Congress, the Executive and Judicial officers of a State, or the members of the Legislature thereof, is denied to any of the male inhabitants of such State, being twenty-one years of age,{14} and citizens of the United States, or in any way abridged, except for participation in rebellion, or other crime, the basis of representation therein shall be reduced in the proportion which the number of such male citizens shall bear to the whole number of male citizens twenty-one years of age in such State.

Section 3—No person shall be a Senator or Representative in Congress, or elector of President and Vice President, or hold any office, civil or military, under the United States, or under any State, who, having previously taken an oath, as a member of Congress, or as an officer of the United States, or as a member of any State legislature, or as an executive or judicial officer of any State, to support the Constitution of the United States, shall have engaged in insurrection or rebellion against the same, or given aid or comfort to the enemies thereof. But Congress may by a vote of two-thirds of each House, remove such disability.

Section 4—The validity of the public debt of the United States, authorized by law, including debts incurred for payment of pensions and bounties for services in suppressing insurrection or rebellion, shall not be questioned. But neither the United States nor any State shall assume or pay any debt or obligation incurred in aid of insurrection or rebellion against the United States, or any claim for the loss or emancipation of any slave; but all such debts, obligations and claims shall be held illegal and void.

Section 5—The Congress shall have power to enforce, by appropriate legislation, the provisions of this article.

Amendment XV [1870] *Section 1*—The right of citizens of the United States to vote shall not be denied or abridged by the United States or by any State on account of race, color, or previous condition of servitude.

Section 2—The Congress shall have power to enforce this article by appropriate legislation.

Amendment XVI [1913] The Congress shall have power to lay and collect taxes on incomes, from whatever source derived, without apportionment among the several States, and without regard to any census or enumeration.

Amendment [XVII] [1913] The Senate of the United States shall be composed of two Senators from each State, elected by the people thereof, for six years; and each Senator shall have one vote. The electors in each State shall have the qualifications requisite for electors of the most numerous branch of the State legislatures.

When vacancies happen in the representation of any State in the Senate, the executive authority of such State shall issue writs of election to fill such vacancies: *Provided,* That the legislature of any State may empower the executive thereof to make temporary appointments until the people fill the vacancies by election as the legislature may direct.

This amendment shall not be so construed as to affect the election or term of any Senator chosen before it becomes valid as part of the Constitution.

Amendment [XVIII] [1919]{15} *Section 1*—After one year from the ratification of this article the manufacture, sale, or transportation of intoxicating liquors within, the importation thereof into, or the exportation thereof from the United States and all territory subject to the jurisdiction thereof for beverage purposes is hereby prohibited.

Section 2—The Congress and the several States shall have concurrent power to enforce this article by appropriate legislation.

Section 3—This article shall be inoperative unless it shall have been ratified as an amendment to the Constitution by the legislatures of the several States, as provided in the Constitution, within seven years from the date of the submission hereof to the States by the Congress.

Amendment [XIX] [1920] The right of citizens of the United States to vote shall not be denied or abridged by the United States or by any State on account of sex.

Congress shall have power to enforce this article by appropriate legislation.

Amendment [XX] [1933] *Section 1*—The terms of the President and Vice President shall end at noon on the 20th day of January, and the terms of Senators and Representatives at noon on the 3d day of January, of the years in which such terms would have ended if this article had not been ratified; and the terms of their successors shall then begin.

Section 2—The Congress shall assemble at least once in every year, and such meeting shall begin at noon on the 3d day of January, unless they shall by law appoint a different day.

Section 3—[16]If, at the time fixed for the beginning of the term of the President, the President elect shall have died, the Vice President elect shall become President. If a President shall not have been chosen before the time fixed for the beginning of his term, or if the President elect shall have failed to qualify, then the Vice President elect shall act as President until a President shall have qualified; and the Congress may by law provide for the case wherein neither a President elect nor a Vice President elect shall have qualified, declaring who shall then act as President, or the manner in which one who is to act shall be selected, and such person shall act accordingly until a President or Vice President shall have qualified.

Section 4—The Congress may by law provide for the case of the death of any of the persons from whom the House of Representatives may choose a President whenever the right of choice shall have devolved upon them, and for the case of the death of any of the persons from whom the Senate may choose a Vice President whenever the right of choice shall have devolved upon them.

Section 5—Sections 1 and 2 shall take effect on the 15th day of October following the ratification of this article.

Section 6—This article shall be inoperative unless it shall have been ratified as an amendment to the Constitution by the legislatures of three-fourths of the several States within seven years from the date of its submission.

Amendment [XXI] [1933] *Section 1*—The eighteenth article of amendment to the Constitution of the United States is hereby repealed.

Section 2—The transportation or importation into any State, Territory, or possession of the United States for delivery or use therein of intoxicating liquors, in violation of the laws thereof, is hereby prohibited.

Section 3—This article shall be inoperative unless it shall have been ratified as an amendment to the Constitution by conventions in the several States, as provided in the Constitution, within seven years from the date of the submission hereof to the States by the Congress.

Amendment [XXII] [1951] *Section 1*—No person shall be elected to the office of the President more than twice, and no person who has held the office of President, or acted as President, for more than two years of a term to which some other person was elected President shall be elected to the office of the President more than once. But this Article shall not apply to any person holding the office of President when this Article was proposed by the Congress, and shall not prevent any person who may be holding the office of President, or acting as President, during the term within which this Article becomes operative from holding the office of President or acting as President during the remainder of such term.

Section 2—This article shall be inoperative unless it shall have been ratified as an amendment to the

Constitution by the legislatures of three-fourths of the several States within seven years from the date of its submission to the States by the Congress.

Amendment [XXIII] [1961] *Section 1*—The District constituting the seat of Government of the United States shall appoint in such manner as the Congress may direct: A number of electors of President and Vice President equal to the whole number of Senators and Representatives in Congress to which the District would be entitled if it were a State, but in no event more than the least populous State; they shall be in addition to those appointed by the States, but they shall be considered, for the purposes of the election of President and Vice President, to be electors appointed by a State; and they shall meet in the District and perform such duties as provided by the twelfth article of amendment.

Section 2—The Congress shall have power to enforce this article by appropriate legislation.

Amendment [XXIV] [1964] *Section 1*—The right of citizens of the United States to vote in any primary or other election for President or Vice President, for electors for President or Vice President, or for Senator or Representative in Congress, shall not be denied or abridged by the United States or any State by reason of failure to pay any poll tax or other tax.

Section 2—The Congress shall have power to enforce this article by appropriate legislation.

Amendment [XXV] [1967] *Section 1*—In case of the removal of the President from office or of his death or resignation, the Vice President shall become President.

Section 2—Whenever there is a vacancy in the office of the Vice President, the President shall nominate a Vice President who shall take office upon confirmation by a majority vote of both Houses of Congress.

Section 3—Whenever the President transmits to the President pro tempore of the Senate and the Speaker of the House of Representatives his written declaration that he is unable to discharge the powers and duties of his office, and until he transmits to them a written declaration to the contrary, such powers and duties shall be discharged by the Vice President as Acting President.

Section 4—Whenever the Vice President and a majority of either the principal officers of the executive departments or of such other body as Congress may by law provide, transmit to the President pro tempore of the Senate and the Speaker of the House of Representatives their written declaration that the President is unable to discharge the powers and duties of his office, the Vice President shall immediately assume the powers and duties of the office as Acting President.

Thereafter, when the President transmits to the President pro tempore of the Senate and the Speaker of the House of Representatives his written declaration that no inability exists, he shall resume the powers and duties of his office unless the Vice President and a majority of either the principal officers of the executive department or of such other body as Congress may by law provide, transmit within four days to the President pro tempore of the Senate and the Speaker of the House of Representatives their written declaration that the President is unable to discharge the powers and duties of his office. Thereupon Congress shall decide the issue, assembling within forty-eight hours for that purpose if not in session. If the Congress, within twenty-one days after receipt of the latter written declaration, or, if Congress is not in session, within twenty-one days after Congress is required to assemble, determines by two-thirds vote of both Houses that the President is unable to discharge the powers and duties of his office, the Vice President shall continue to discharge the same as Acting President; otherwise, the President shall resume the powers and duties of his office.

Amendment [XXVI] [1971] *Section 1*—The right of citizens of the United States, who are eighteen years of age or older, to vote shall not be denied or abridged by the United States or by any State on account of age.

Section 2—The Congress shall have power to enforce this article by appropriate legislation.

Amendment [XXVII] [1992] No law, varying the compensation for the services of the Senators and Representatives, shall take effect, until an election of Representatives shall have intervened.

NOTES

1. This text of the Constitution follows the engrossed copy signed by General Washington and the deputies from 12 states. The superior number preceding the paragraphs designates the number of the clause; it was not in the original.
2. The part included in brackets was changed by section 2 of the 14th amendment.
3. The part included in brackets was changed by section 1 of the 17th amendment.
4. The part included in brackets was changed by clause 2 of the 17th amendment.
5. The part included in brackets was changed by section 2 of the 20th amendment.
6. See also the 16th amendment.
7. This paragraph has been superseded by the 12th amendment.
8. This provision has been affected by the 25th amendment.

9. This clause has been affected by the 11th amendment.{
10. This paragraph has been superseded by the 13th amendment.
11. Obsolete.
12. Only Amendments XIII, XIV, XV, and XVI had numbers assigned to them at the time of ratification.
13. The part included in brackets has been superseded by section 3 of Amendment XX.
14. (See Amendment XXVI.
15. Repealed by section 1 of Amendment XXI.
16. See Amendment XXV.

Glossary

abridge To diminish (as a right) by reducing or shortening in scope.

abrogate To abolish or do away with by an official act.

acquittal An acknowledgment by a court of law of the innocence of the defendant or defendants.

adjudication The act or process of judicially settling a matter.

bicameral Consisting of two legislative bodies.

bill of attainder In English law, a legislative act attainting (that is, nullifying the civil rights of) a person without trial.

carpetbagger Word coined in the Reconstruction period (1865–77) to describe a Northerner (with belongings in a carpetbag) in the South to seek private gain.

common law Body of English law based on custom and general principles and that, embodied in case law, serves as precedent or is applied to situations not covered by statute.

cornucopia An inexhaustible store; abundance.

coup de grace A decisive finishing blow that puts an end to something.

coup d'état The violent overthrow or alteration of an existing government by a small group.

de facto Existing as a matter of fact, without lawful authority.

delimit To fix or define the limits of.

doctrine A statement of fundamental government policy, especially in international relations.

eminent domain Government power to take private property for public use without the owner's consent.

ex post facto Having retroactive force.

Freedman's Bureau (1865–72) U.S. agency established during Reconstruction to help freed slaves in their transition to freedom.

Glorious Revolution In English history, the Revolution of 1688– 89 is known as both the Glorious Revolution and the Bloodless Revolution because the monarch, James II, was toppled from his throne without a war.

indictment A formal written statement framed by a prosecuting authority and found by a jury (as a grand jury) charging a person with an offense.

jurisprudence A body or system of law; the philosophy of law.

larceny The unlawful taking of personal property with intent to deprive the rightful owner of it permanently.

levy To impose or collect by legal authority.

litigant One engaged in a lawsuit.

Magna Carta Latin for "great charter," the Magna Carta states the liberties guaranteed to the English people by King John in 1215, proclaiming rights that have become a part of English law and are now the foundation of the constitution of every English-speaking nation.

negligent Careless; neglectful.

nullification In U.S. history, the doctrine upholding the right of a state to declare null and void within its boundaries an act of the federal government.

palladium Something that affords effectual protection or security; safeguard.

partisan A firm adherent to a party, faction, cause, or person; especially: one exhibiting blind, prejudiced, and unreasoning allegiance.

peyote A stimulant hallucinogenic drug containing mescaline that is derived from peyote buttons and used especially in the religious ceremonies of some American Indian peoples.

poll tax A fixed (rather than graduated) tax per head levied on adults, the payment of which is made a requirement for voting.

presentment The act of presenting to an authority a formal statement of a matter to be dealt with.

promulgate To declare; to set forth publicly.

proscription An imposed restraint, restriction, or prohibition.

pro tempore Latin phrase literally meaning "for the time being." When applied to an office or legislative position, it denotes one individual who assumes the responsibilities of another in his or her absence.

quartering Providing room and board for soldiers in private homes.

quorum The minimum number of members of a legislative body that must be present for business to officially be conducted.

referendum The practice of submitting to popular vote a measure passed on or proposed by a legislative body or by popular initiative.

sacramental Of or relating to sacred rites.

salient Prominent; noticeable.

scalawag Name for a white Southerner who had opposed secession and later supported the Reconstruction governments.

secular Not overtly or specifically religious.

temperance A movement dedicated to promoting moderation and, more often, complete abstinence in the use of intoxicating liquor.

titular Holding an office in title or name only (without the duties, functions, or responsibilities).

vest To grant or endow with something, such as power or rights.

void Of no legal force or effect.

vote of no confidence A procedure used by members of a legislative body (generally the lower house in a bicameral system) to defeat or weaken a government.

writ of habeas corpus From Medieval Latin, literally, you should have the body, a formal written document asserting that when a person is held prisoner, a judge may compel the jailer to bring the prisoner to court and explain why he or she is being held captive. If no lawful reason is found, the prisoner must be released.

Bibliography

THE U.S. CONSTITUTION

A good general work on the U.S. Constitution is Edward S. Corwin, *Edward S. Corwin's The Constitution and What It Means Today*, rev. by Harold W. Chase and *Craig R. Ducat*, 14th ed. (1978). Leonard W. Levy and Kenneth L. Karst (eds.), *Encyclopedia of the American Constitution*, 2nd ed., 6 vol. (2000), is a comprehensive, multidisciplinary reference work. Historical discussions include Carl Brent Swisher, *American Constitutional Development*, 2nd ed. (1954, reprinted 1978); and Philip B. Kurland and Ralph Lerner (eds.), *The Founders' Constitution*, 5 vol. (1987, reissued 2000), a monumental collection of 17th-, 18th-, and 19th-century documents that bear on all parts of the Constitution.

CONSTITUTIONAL LAW

A helpful place to begin for background on the national legal and judicial systems that provide the foundations for constitutional law and judicial review is Herbert M. Kritzer (ed.), *Legal Systems of the World: A Political, Social, and Cultural Encyclopedia* (2002). A comprehensive study of variations in the constitutional forms of democracies may be found in Arend Lijphart, *Patterns of Democracy: Government Forms and Performance in Thirty-six Countries* (1999).

General works on American constitutional law include Laurence H. Tribe, *American Constitutional Law*, 3rd ed. (2000); and Lee Epstein and Thomas G. Walker,

Constitutional Law for a Changing America: Institutional Powers and Constraints, 5th ed. (2004), and *Constitutional Law for a Changing America: Rights, Liberties, and Justice*, 5th ed. (2004).

An analysis of constitutional law in the British Commonwealth is Leslie Zines, *Constitutional Change in the Commonwealth* (1991). Surveys of individual countries include Hamid Khan, *Constitutional and Political History of Pakistan* (2001); Peter C. Oliver, *The Constitution of Independence: The Development of Constitutional Theory in Australia, Canada, and New Zealand* (2005); and A.W. Bradley and K.D. Ewing, *Constitutional and Administrative Law*, 13th ed. (2003), a classic on Great Britain's constitution. Judicial review in the United States is discussed in Robert G. McCloskey, *The American Supreme Court*, 4th ed., rev. by *Sanford Levinson* (2005). A useful symposium on comparative judicial review is Donald W. Jackson and C. Neal Tate (eds.), *Comparative Judicial Review and Public Policy* (1992). An authoritative analysis of judicial review as an institution and of the constitutional law produced by it is Mauro Cappelletti, *Judicial Review in the Contemporary World* (1971).

Index

K

L

M

N

O

P

Q

R

S

T

U

V

W